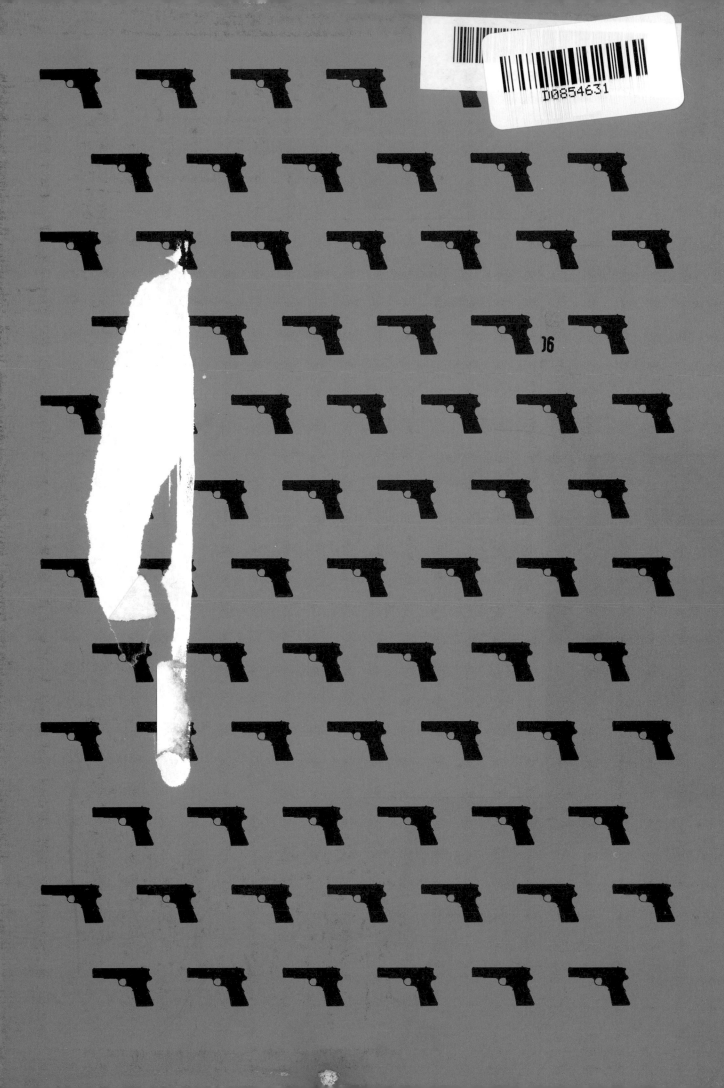

SECRET WAR

CAXTON EDITIONS
AN IMPRINT OF CAXTON PUBLISHING GROUP
20 BLOOMSBURY STREET, LONDON WC1 3QA

© CAXTON EDITIONS, 2001

ISBN 1-84067-291-9

A COPY OF THE CIP DATA IS AVAILABLE FROM THE
BRITISH LIBRARY UPON REQUEST.

DESIGNED AND PRODUCED FOR CAXTON EDITIONS
BY KEITH POINTING DESIGN CONSULTANCY

REPROGRAPHICS BY GA GRAPHICS
PRINTED AND BOUND
BY SUN FUNG OFFSET BINDING CO LTD

COPY EDITOR SASHA BEHAR

SECRET WAR

A PICTORIAL RECORD OF THE
SPECIAL OPERATIONS EXECUTIVE

TEXT BY
JULIETTE PATTINSON

CAXTON EDITIONS

CHAPTER 1

SETTING EUROPE ABLAZE

In 1938, when war seemed inevitable, an organisation called MI R (Military Intelligence, Research) was established. Headed by Colonel JFC Holland and Sir Colin Gubbins, who later became the Executive Head of SOE, MI R studied various techniques of irregular warfare, such as guerrilla tactics and paramilitary operations, and concluded in the summer of 1939 that guerrilla warfare could assist in diverting enemy troops if used in conjunction with the regular armed forces.

As a result, the Special Operations Executive was created on 1 July 1940. Its establishment was an experiment: a desperate attempt to respond to the Nazi blitzkrieg ('lightning war') and the capitulation of France in June 1940, following the Dunkirk debacle. SOE was a product of the period when Britain stood alone and its existence brought to an end the weeks of inactivity known as the Phoney War.

LEFT: *Winston Churchill inspecting a Tommy gun on 31 July 1940. SOE had been in existence for just 30 days.*

Although the Phoney War period witnessed acts of sabotage and subversion, these were isolated incidents and were afforded a low priority by the War Office. The new strategy was a product of Churchill's romanticism which was fuelled by his memories of quasi-guerrilla fighting on the north-west frontier and in South Africa.

Sabotage and subversion were given increased prominence in Churchill's war strategy. A Chiefs of Staff discussion on 'British Strategy in a Certain Eventuality' stated:

> 'We regard this form of activity as of the very highest importance. A special organisation will be required and plans to put these operations into effect should be prepared, and all the necessary preparations and training should be proceeded with as a matter of urgency.'

The SOE Charter, laying down its tasks and functions, declared that this new organisation would 'co-ordinate all action, by way of subversion and sabotage, against the enemy overseas'. SOE acted as a catalyst, increasing the pace of resistance against the Nazi regime, by sending in trained men and women to recruit, instruct and arm local resisters, by establishing communications networks, by arranging parachute drops and Lysander pick-ups and by planning sabotage operations.

Hugh Dalton, the Minister of Economic Warfare, recognised the need for a guerrilla movement. In a letter to Lord Halifax, Dalton wrote:

> 'We have got to organise movements in enemy-occupied territory comparable to the Sinn Fein movement in Ireland, to the Chinese Guerrillas now operating against Japan, to the Spanish Irregulars who played a notable part in Wellington's

campaign or – one might as well admit it – to the organisations which the Nazis themselves have developed so remarkably in almost every country in the world...It is quite clear to me that an organisation on this scale and of this character is not something which can be handled by the ordinary departmental machinery of either the British Civil Service or the British military machine. What is needed is a new organisation to co-ordinate, inspire, control and assist the nationals of the oppressed countries who must themselves be the direct participants...The organisation should, in my view, be entirely independent of the War Office machine.'

The Ministry of Economic Warfare was regarded as a suitable cover for the new organisation and Dalton was chosen as the Ministerial Head of SOE. Dalton appointed Sir Frank Nelson as the Executive Head to run it. There were some replacements in these positions and Colin Gubbins assumed the position of Executive Head.

ABOVE: *Major-General Colin Gubbins pictured in uniform whilst he worked in MI R.*

EXECUTIVE HEADS OF SOE

  1. Sir Frank Nelson ....July 40 - May 42

  2. Sir Charles Hambro ....May 42 - Sept.43

  3. Major-General Colin Gubbins..........Sept. 43 - June 46

Each of the three Executive Heads, Nelson, Hambro and

Gubbins, took the symbol CD.

MINISTERIAL HEADS OF SOE

  1. Hugh Dalton ....July 40 - Feb. 42

  2. Lord Selborne ....Feb. 42 - June 46

SOE was divided into country sections, each with its own staff.
France was unique in that there were four sections operational
there: RF, F, EU/P and DF. RF (République Française) was run by
the French and was pro-Gaullist, F was British-run, EU/P was
Polish-run and DF was the escape line organisation.

SOE initially operated from a remote part of Newmarket
Racecourse. By the end of October 1940, the different country
sections began moving into offices in Baker Street and by the
beginning of 1944, most of one side of Baker Street had been
requisitioned by SOE. By February 1942, SOE also had officers in

Marks and Spencer's Michaelhouse and its adjacent properties, Berkeley, Chiltern and Orchard Courts and Bicknell Mansions. Orchard Court in Portman Square was used by F section. It was here that the agents were briefed about their mission.

ABOVE: *Maurice Buckmaster, head of F section.*

BELOW RIGHT: *64 Baker Street, F section's headquarters.*

BELOW LEFT: *85 Baker Street.*

CHAPTER 2

RECRUITMENT & TRAINING

The first recruiting officer for F section was Lewis Gielgud, the brother of the actor, John Gielgud. Initially, there were no female agents in France because lawyers in SOE believed that by recruiting women agents, they would be contravening the Geneva Convention, which stated that women could not bear arms. It was considered highly controversial and it was not until late 1942, when Selwyn Jepson replaced Lewis Gielgud, that women began to be conscripted.

'I was responsible for recruiting women for the work, in the face of a good deal of opposition from the powers that be, who said that women, under the Geneva Convention, were not allowed to take combatant duties (which they regarded resistance work in France as being).'

LEFT: *Students during training being shown how to aim a gun. Taken from the film 'Now It Can Be Told'.*

Although the Dutch and Belgian sections sent in a couple of women agents, it was really only in France that women were operational in a substantial number. 40 women were sent to France by F section, the British branch run by Maurice Buckmaster, and RF infiltrated a further 12.

Interviews were held in either the War Office or a bedroom converted into an office at the Hotel Victoria in Northumberland Avenue. They were invariably held in French and lasted about 20 minutes. If the candidate was accepted, they were sent onto a series of training schools.

SOE commandeered numerous secluded country estates, far away from prying eyes, and these were used as training schools. Each school had a number and was prefixed by the initials STS, standing for Special Training School. For example, Arisaig House, in Arisaig, Inverness-shire was known as STS 21. At each stage, students, as the recruits were known, were assessed: those that were considered suitable graduated to the next course; those that failed to impress were sent back to their original units, having been reminded that they had signed the Official Secrets Act.

The first training school that the students attended was Wanborough Manor near Guildford, Surrey. This preliminary course lasted about two to four weeks and if the individual successfully passed this first hurdle, they then went to the para-military course which lasted between three and five weeks. This was much tougher than the initial course and was held in what was known as a Group A Special Training School. One of these was stationed at Arisaig, a rugged area on the western coast

ABOVE: *Wanborough Manor, near Guildford in Surrey.*

of Inverness. Here, they were trained in survival skills, such as fieldcraft and map work, as well as being taught unarmed combat and silent killing. The agents also underwent sabotage training, learning how to blow up railway bridges and locomotives with plastic explosive. A poacher taught them how to live off the land and they were shown how to load, aim and fire different weapons.

From Arisaig, they moved onto Ringway, which is now Manchester airport. This was where they were taught how to parachute. They began by jumping out of the fuselage of a grounded plane, then progressed to jumping out of a plane during the day and at night and finally, jumping from a stationary barrage balloon which most agents intensely disliked.

Roger Landes, an F section agent, recalled his parachute training at Ringway:

> 'During our training, we used to jump from a lorry doing 30 miles an hour and learn how to roll on our

shoulder, because you touch the ground at 30 miles an hour. We dropped from 500 feet and the parachute opened automatically within two and a half seconds and then it took half a minute to touch the ground. When you see the parachute open, you always look up. Then you have to learn how to fall on the ground. During the training, someone with a loudspeaker on the ground used to say "keep your legs together" because if you keep your feet apart, you may break a leg. And when you touch the ground, you roll on your shoulder. We also jumped from a balloon. Instead of jumping from 500 feet, the balloon was at 1,000 feet and instead of opening in two and a half seconds, the parachute opens in five seconds. We jumped during the day with very bad sunglasses, because the weather was too bad to jump at night. When you leave the plane, you are doing up to about 200 miles an hour. The normal speed, when you sail down, is 69 miles an hour. I had five jumps in training.'

Having undertaken the parachute jumping, the students then moved onto the Group B schools which were situated on Lord Montagu's estate at Beaulieu in the New Forest, Hampshire. There were twelve secluded country houses on the estate in which the students lived. Beaulieu is better known today as a motor museum and most members of the public are unlikely to have heard of its secret past during the war, when about 3,000 individuals passed through its doors. This final course was known as the Finishing School and prepared the students for living a clandestine life. They were taught how to look inconspicuous, use secret inks, undertake forgery, accomplish safe-blowing, as well as being taught to recognise different German uniforms. During the night, each individual was brusquely shaken awake and marched to an office, flanked by staff of the training schools dressed in Gestapo uniform. They were then subjected to a mock interrogation to test how well they endured questioning.

At the end of their training, the recruits were sent on a scheme which lasted about four days, in which they had to accomplish various tasks. They were able to put into practice what they had learnt at the various training schools.

After each student was allocated a role, either that of organiser, liaison officer (courier), wireless operator, arms instructor or saboteur, they were then sent on various courses to hone specific skills. There were courses on arranging reception committees, sabotage, Morse and coding. Wireless operating was the most complex training and students allocated to this role underwent much longer training than those sent in as couriers or organisers.

CHAPTER 3

INDIVIDUAL AGENTS & GEORGE CROSS HOLDERS

Over 400 agents were sent into France by F section, 39 of whom were women. Some of the female recruits were civilians, whilst others were from the WAAF (Women's Auxiliary Air Force) and the ATS (Auxiliary Territorial Service). The recruits were of varied age, ranging from early twenties to mid-forties. They came from a variety of occupational backgrounds: from the professions, (teaching, nursing, secretarial and journalism); from the leisure industries, (there was a beauty queen and a beautician); from the entertainment sector, (there were actresses and actors, motor-racers and artists); as well as shop assistants and hairdressers. There were a variety of nationalities represented,

LEFT: *Odette Sansom.*

including Mauritian, Swiss, Australian, Chilean, Polish, American and Russian and many were Anglo-French. They also came from a variety of religious backgrounds; there were Jews, devout Roman Catholics and a Sufi. Some had initially been pacifists, but judged the fight against Nazism to be a just War.

A handful of agents were awarded the George Cross. Established by King George VI, it is a British civilian and military decoration for 'acts of the greatest heroism or of the most conspicuous courage in circumstances of extreme danger'. Only four women have been directly awarded the George Cross, three for their work with SOE (conferred posthumously on Violette Szabo and Noor Inayat Khan and presented to Odette Sansom).

Odette Sansom

Odette is perhaps the most famous of the women agents. Born Odette Brailly, she married an Englishman and had three daughters. She was recruited into SOE as a liaison officer, given the code-name 'Lise' and was smuggled into France on board a fishing vessel in the autumn of 1942. She was captured by Hugo Bleicher, an Abwehr agent posing as a defector. She spent many months in Fresnes prison on the outskirts of Paris. Initially, she was taken daily to Gestapo Headquarters at the rue des Saussaies for interrogation. She was badly tortured; a red-hot poker was placed on the third vertebrae of her spine and each of her ten toenails were extracted. When it became clear that she was not going to divulge any information, Odette Sansom was deported to Ravensbrück concentration camp for women, where she was placed in solitary confinement in a cell near the wall where executions occurred. She was left for three months and eleven days in complete darkness as punishment. On another occasion, she was left without food for ten days. Despite being in solitary confinement for two years, she managed to occupy her mind by mentally redecorating the houses of people she knew and making clothes for her three daughters.

Odette Sansom was eager to keep mentally healthy and believed that by retaining her smart appearance, she would boost her spirit. Each day, she turned her dark grey skirt an inch so that it wouldn't be worn in one place. She used the shreds from her silk stockings and put them in her hair as curlers every night. Despite not being able to wear shoes after her ordeal, she was determined to wear them when she was ordered to see the Commandant. During her confinement, she kept up the pretence that she was married to Winston Churchill's nephew. Her organiser was called Peter Churchill and they did marry after the war, but he was no relation to the Prime Minster. Nevertheless, this pretence gave both Odette Sansom and Peter Churchill some bargaining power and immediately prior to the liberation of Ravensbrück concentration camp, the Camp Commandant, Fritz Sühren, took her with him as he left the camp to meet the advancing Americans in the vain hope that she would be able to save him. She didn't; he was captured, tried and executed as a war criminal.

She was awarded the George Cross for her behaviour during the two years of imprisonment. A film was made of her wartime experiences simply called *Odette* in which Anna Neagle played the title role. Odette Sansom spent a year with the actress, revisiting the places in which she operated and was imprisoned. She spent the rest of her life keeping the memory alive of the other women agents who did not return.

'What you have to do is remember because it is a
duty one has to one's comrades, to all the good and
brave people. You have to remember them. I'm only

extremely sad and always will be for the rest of my life that my comrades did not come back. I did survive and I know I should not have. I don't take any pride in that. It's nothing to do with me whatsoever.'

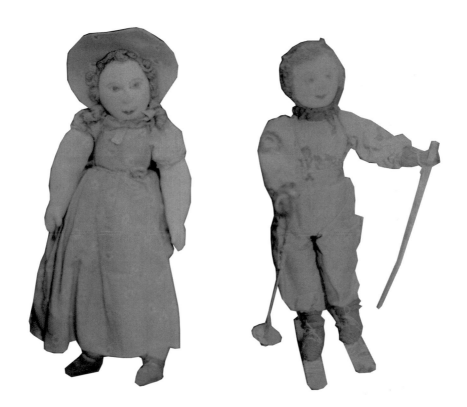

ABOVE: *Whilst in captivity in Fresnes prison, Odette Sansom made rag dolls to pass the time. One she dressed in a skiing outfit and another in a dress. She gave the dolls to a German padre who kept them until the end of the war when he returned them to her.*

Violette Szabo

Born Violette Bushell, to a French mother and an English father, Violette married a Hungarian who was killed at El Alamein. Before joining the ATS, she had worked behind the counter at Woolworths. She joined SOE as a liaison agent becoming 'Louise', and during her training used to go to the local shooting galleries to play for cigarettes. Cyril Watney, an SOE agent who trained with her, recalls:

> 'We went nearly every evening. She said "Do you want some cigarettes?" because you couldn't get cigarettes during the war at one time, they were rationed and so she said "I'll shoot for cigarettes." Between Piccadilly Circus and Leicester Square there was a shooting range, so we went there. It was on the first floor so we went up, they all seemed to know her and they said "Do you want sixpence worth?" So she took sixpence worth and she cut the bull's-eye out, just like that, bang, bang, bang and they gave her the cigarettes.'

LEFT: *Violette Szabo.*

During her parachute training at Ringway, Violette Szabo injured her left foot. This was to have far-reaching consequences when she was evading capture. She was ambushed during her second mission and when trying to escape across fields with Jacques Dufour, she further sprained her weak ankle and could no longer run. She took position behind a tree and started to fire on the advancing German soldiers, whilst Dufour escaped. She was captured and after interrogation at Fresnes, was sent to Ravensbrück concentration camp. She was sent on a work transport before being executed as a terrorist along with fellow SOE agents Denise Bloch and Lilian Rolfe on 5 February 1945.

The George Cross, which was posthumously awarded to her, was collected by her four year old daughter Tania. A film was made about Violette's wartime work with SOE called *Carve Her Name With Pride*, with Virginia McKenna playing the title role.

ABOVE: *Despite being only 20, Jacques Dufour, codenamed 'Anastasie', was a leading figure in the Haute Vienne maquis and had been named as 'the greatest bandit in the Limoges area' by the Gestapo. He was with Violette Szabo when she was ambushed by German soldiers, but managed to escape.*

Noor Inayat Khan

Noor-un-nisa Inayat Khan, meaning 'Light of Womanhood', was born in the Kremlin, Moscow in 1914. Her father was the head of a Sufi sect and her mother was American. Before the war, she had written children's stories which were broadcast on Radio Paris. She was the first woman sent to France as a wireless operator. With the increasing number of wireless operators being arrested, 'Madeleine's' workload escalated. She worked through-out the day and night encoding and decoding, transmitting and delivering messages. In October 1943, a woman called Renée contacted the local Gestapo and gave them Noor Inayat Khan's address. Subsequently, she was arrested and Renée was rewarded with 100,000 francs. Noor Inayat Khan was taken to 84 Avenue Foch, the counter espionage HQ where she immediately tried to escape. She was recaptured and after a subsequent attempted escape, which also ended in failure, she was sent to Pforzheim prison in Germany. She remained there for almost ten months, in which time she was kept in solitary confinement and in chains. Nevertheless, she did manage to make contact with three Frenchwomen who were in a nearby cell.

LEFT: *Noor Inayat Khan.*

ABOVE: *Noor Inayat Khan in traditional Indian dress, playing the vina. This is an Indian stringed musical instrument which resembled the guitar.*

One of the women decided to see if there were any other French people in the prison and scratched on her mess tin using a knitting needle: 'Here are three Frenchwomen.' The mess tin was taken away to be cleaned and when it was returned, carried the reply: 'You are not alone. You have a friend. Cell No 1.' The contact between Noor Inayat Khan in cell No 1 and the three women in cell No 12 continued for a few months. Yvonne

Yolande La Grave, the only occupant of cell 12 who survived the war, stated: 'in the course of our correspondence, she let us know that she was unhappy, very unhappy, that she never went out, that her hands and feet were manacled, that except when they brought us soup or changed our water they never opened her cell door, or the small opening through which they made us pass our mess tins; that they waited until there was no one in the passage and the people who carried the saucepans had passed.' In mid-September 1944, the message 'I am going' was written hastily on the mess tin.

She was taken with Yolande Beekman, Eliane Plewman and Madeleine Damerment to Dachau concentration camp on 12 September 1944. They were forced to kneel in pairs. Whilst holding hands, they were shot in the back of the head. Noor Inayat Khan was posthumously awarded the *Croix de Guerre* by the French, and the British bestowed upon her the *George Cross*. Although only three agents received the George Cross, there were many other outstanding agents who received recognition for their wartime work. In the following pages, the stories of just some of them are told.

BELOW: *Some of the medals awarded to SOE agents.*

TOP ROW: *(left to right): DSO (Distinguished Service Order) and the British Empire (Military) medal.*

BOTTOM ROW: *(left to right): The Croix de Guerre, Médaille de la Résistance Francaise and the Médaille des Forces Francaises Libres.*

Yvonne Baseden

Yvonne Baseden, the daughter of a French mother and British father, joined the WAAF and was recruited by F section as a wireless operator. Codenamed 'Odette', she parachuted into Toulouse in March 1944 to the SCHOLAR circuit. Her group received the first daylight drop of arms after D-Day called Operation Cadillac and recovered 3,783 containers.

Throughout the operation, she was sitting in a ditch in contact with London. In the evening, the group was celebrating in a safe house, a cheese factory in Dôle, when German soldiers arrived. One by one, they were forced from their hiding places and taken to the local prison. Yvonne Baseden was moved to Dijon prison, where she was mistreated, and then onto Ravensbrück concentration camp where she met up with her SOE friends, Violette Szabo, Denise Bloch and Lilian Rolfe. She was put on the last Red Cross transport and taken to Sweden. Her survival resulted from the fact that she was never identified as an SOE agent.

Francis Cammaerts

Francis Cammaerts was a conscientious objector but the death of his brother in the RAF and his decision that this was a just war prompted him into action. He joined F section as an organiser and was sent to work with Odette Sansom and Peter Churchill in the south of France in March 1943. He decided that their contact with a German defector,

which was eventually to lead to their arrest, was unsafe and left to form his own circuit called JOCKEY. As 'Roger', he became a highly successful and well-respected organiser.

He was arrested at a routine road block after the Liberation, when the serial numbers on his francs were found to be in sequence with those of a fellow traveller whom he said he did not know. The day before he was to be executed, his courier 'Pauline', the Polish heiress Christine Granville, bribed the local German Officer. As a result, Cammaerts was released and after the war, resumed his job as a schoolteacher.

Nancy Wake

An Australian woman who married a Marseilles industrialist, Nancy Wake became involved in an escape route network which assisted Allied soldiers across the Pyrenees to neutral Spain. She used her own escape line to evade capture  and when she got to London, joined F section as a liaison agent. As 'Hélène', she worked with the maquis in the Auvergne district of France, participated in a raid on a Gestapo headquarters and was involved in battles with SS troops. She was awarded the George Medal, the Croix de Guerre with Palm and Bar, the Croix de Guerre with Star, the Medaille de la Resistance, the American Medal of Freedom with Bronze Palm and was made a Chevalier de la Légion d'Honneur. In 1949, Nancy entered politics as a Liberal Candidate and she only narrowly missed becoming Prime Minister of Australia. She received only 127 votes less than Dr Herbert de Vere Evatt, the leader of the Australian Labour Party.

Yvonne Cormeau

Yvonne Cormeau parachuted to a field near Bordeaux on 22/23 August 1943 and worked as a wireless operator in Gascony to the WHEELWRIGHT circuit. In the 13 months that she was operational, Cormeau, code-named 'Annette', sent over 400 messages to London. She became such a nuisance to the Germans that 'Wanted' posters, with an accurate sketch of her, were printed. When she was with the maquis, the Germans attacked and she was wounded in the leg. She was awarded the MBE, the Légion d'Honneur, the Croix de Guerre and the Medaille combattant volontaire de la Résistance.

BELOW: *Her dress which bears the bullet hole, and her bloodstained briefcase.*

Tony Brooks

Tony Brooks, code-name 'Alphonse', was the youngest F section agent at 20 years of age. He was dropped blind (no reception committee present to meet him), landing many miles off target. Trying out a new type of parachute, he landed horizontally in the only tree on the dropping zone, which broke his fall. He was organiser of PIMENTO, a circuit which specialised in railway sabotage around Montaubon and Lyons and his group, mainly cheminots (railway employees) put a whole SS division out of action.

Eileen Nearne

Eileen Nearne, known as Didi, was the younger sister of Jacqueline Nearne, who starred in the SOE film *Now It Can Be Told*, and another SOE agent Francis Nearne. She landed in France, using the code-name 'Rose', on 2 March 1944. She worked as a  WT operator to the WIZARD circuit based in Paris. On 21 July 1944, she had just finished transmitting a message, when German soldiers arrived. She had time to burn her codes and dismantle her set, but her gun was quickly found and she was taken away for interrogation. She was tortured and in September 1944, she was sent to Ravensbrück concentration camp, where she met Violette Szabo, Denise Bloch and Lilian Rolfe. She refused to work in a factory, whereupon guards shaved her head and said she would be shot. She agreed to work and in December 1944 was sent to Markkleeberg, near Leipzig to work on the roads for 12 hours a day. While being moved to another camp, she managed to escape into a forest with two Frenchwomen.

Lise de Baissac

The Nearne's were not the only siblings who belonged to SOE. There were a number of others, including Claude and Lise de Baissac. Lise de Baissac, who trained with Odette Sansom, parachuted into the Loire valley with  Andrée Borrel, (who was executed at Natzweiler concentration camp), on 24 September 1942. Lise had her own tiny circuit called ARTIST in Poitiers and, as 'Odile', she was responsible for receiving agents, passing on contacts and couriering messages. She also acted as liaison officer between the SCIENTIST, PROSPER and BRICKLAYER circuits. She worked with Dericourt (who was later exposed as a double agent) on his first landing operation, in which they received two Lysanders. The operation was a success. As the Liberation approached, she asked for her uniform to be dropped to her so that she could greet the advancing Allied Forces.

Roger Landes

Roger Landes joined SOE as a wireless operator and after three failed attempts to parachute in (the pilot could not locate the dropping zone on the first journey, the wrong signal letter was given on the second and on the third, anti-aircraft gunners fired on them), he finally succeeded on 31 October 1942. Even then, the pilot had to bring the Halifax bomber down to 250 feet – about half the height from which parachutists normally jumped. Codenamed 'Stanislas', he joined Claude de Baissac's SCIENTIST circuit. After his first mission was complete, he returned to London, was debriefed and parachuted back in as an organiser of the ACTOR circuit. He commanded an army of 7,000 maquisards in the Bordeaux area. After the Liberation, he met General de Gaulle in Bordeaux on 17 September 1944. De Gaulle dismissed Landes, saying 'You are British. Your place is not here.' On 21 March 1947, Landes was awarded the Croix de Guerre with Silver Star and a Military Cross with bar.

Denise Bloch

Denise Bloch was a French Jew who arrived in France by Lysander on 2 March 1944. As 'Ambroise', she worked as a wireless operator to the CLERGYMAN circuit. The group was responsible for sabotaging railway lines in Nantes and high pylons which crossed the river Loire. She was captured in a Gestapo raid on 18 June 1944 and sent to Ravensbrück concentration camp with Violette Szabo and Lilian Rolfe. They were sent to Torgau camp, near to Ravensbrück, to work and it is here that they planned an escape. Unfortunately, they were returned to the main camp before these plans came to fruition. Then, in winter, they were sent to Königsberg on a second, much tougher work transport. She was killed, along with Lilian Rolfe and Violette Szabo, by a single shot to the back of the neck on 5 February 1945. After they had been shot, their bodies were taken to the crematorium and burned. The Légion d'Honneur and the Croix de Guerre avec Palme were posthumously conferred upon her.

RIGHT: *Denise Bloch.*

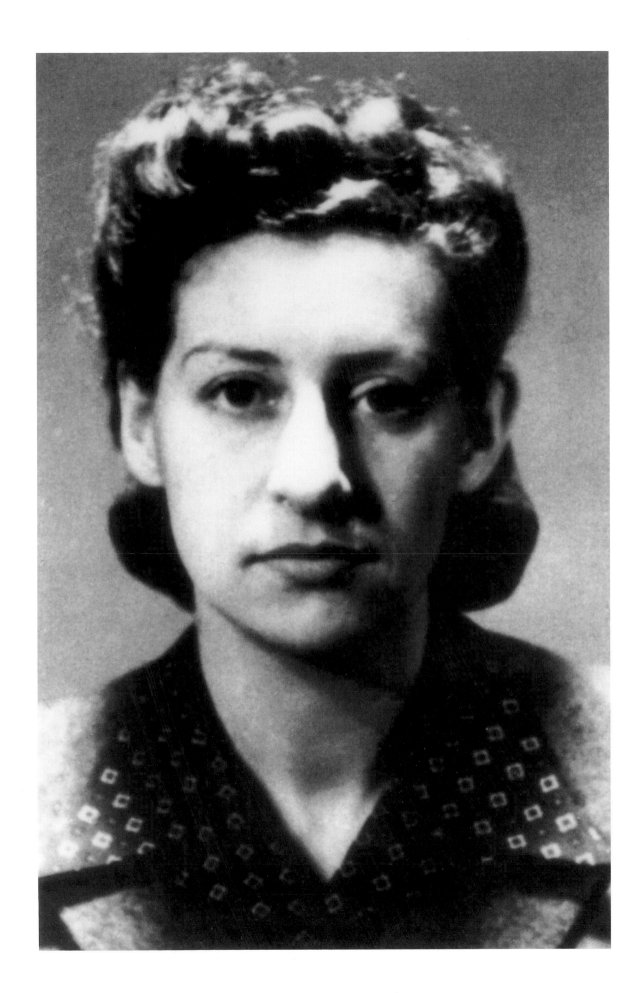

Lilian Rolfe

Lilian Rolfe, a twin, born to a French mother and British father, lived in Brazil and moved to Britain to join the WAAF. She parachuted into France on 5 April 1944 as a wireless operator to the HISTORIAN circuit. Code-named 'Claudie' and 'Nadine', she sent 67 messages to London which were always clear and  accurate despite the large Gestapo presence in the area. She was captured on 30 July 1944, sent to Fresnes prison in Paris and then in August, she was deported to Ravensbrück in Germany. As a result of a forced labour transport, she became very ill with lung trouble which caused breathing difficulties and she could not walk. Sources report that she had to be taken by stretcher to the place of execution on 5 February 1945. Lilian Rolfe was posthumously awarded the Croix de Guerre avec Palme.

ABOVE: *Lilian Rolfe in WAAF uniform.*

RIGHT: *Lilian Rolfe.*

There are very few pictures of agents that were taken during the war. For obvious reasons, the agents did not want to be captured on camera. However, there are some photographs, including this picture of Lilian Rolfe, left in the photograph, which was taken in St. Hilaire, near Orleans, France, in May 1944, shortly before her arrest in July 1944. She is pictured with 14 year old Marty Lejeune, the daughter of Henri Lejeune, the owner of the garage from which Lilian operated her wireless set. When Lilian arrived in France, Marty assisted her in hiding her radio set in the garage. What is interesting about the photograph is that it illustrates the type of clothing and hairstyles that were fashionable in France in the 1940s.

RIGHT: *Lilian Rolfe in St. Hilaire, May 1944 with Marty Lejeune.*

CHAPTER 4

GOING INTO THE FIELD

Before going into the field, SOE headquarters ensured that each agent had false documentation, a cover name, a field name and a well-rehearsed cover story. Without them, the agents were liable to be arrested, deported and executed. Careful consideration had to be given to the place from which the documents were issued, and SOE tried to use the names of towns from which the records had been destroyed by bombing, so they could not be verified. In an attempt to combat resistance and fake documentation, the Germans continually modified ration cards, but F section was kept so well informed of these alterations, that new ration cards were in use within hours of the changes. As well as printing presses in the field, the art department of the 'Thatched Barn' was used to manufacture the forged francs, ration cards and

LEFT: *Still from the SOE film 'Now It Can Be Told'.*

identity cards. Situated on the A1 bypass at Barnet, the Thatched Barn, (Station XV) was designed in the Thirties as one of Britain's first motels. As well as a forgery section, there was a camouflage department which was responsible for adapting clothing. Continental and English styles of clothing were quite dissimilar and a single item of clothing could expose the agent. Styles of collars, cuffs and seams were all different on the Continent and so clothing had to be adapted to European specifications. At the Thatched Barn, seamstresses would ensure that 'Made in England' labels were taken out and replaced with 'Fabriqué en France'. Since new items of clothing and footwear looked suspicious, they had to be aged. This was done by the staff wearing the items whilst they worked so they became creased and scuffed. Accessories, such as bags and wallets, also had to be aged and this was either done by applying various ointments to the leather or simply by kicking them around the workshop.

ABOVE: *Fake clothes labels and German military insignia, manufactured by the Thatched Barn.*

As well as being issued authentic clothing, every agent possessed a number of forged documents, including identity cards, birth certificates, ration cards and travel permits. Agents were continually asked for documentation to verify who they were and were asked numerous questions. This happened on a daily basis: when making a telephone call from public places; when booking a room in a hotel; when ordering food in a restaurant or buying it in a shop and, with increased scrutiny from German soldiers, when they crossed borders and passed checkpoints. Everyday activities like cycling or walking were dangerous because of snap controls. Roads would be routinely closed off, trapping everyone in them, and each person's documents would be examined. Travelling on a train was particularly hazardous as stations were heavily guarded and the Gestapo often did rounds on the trains.

ABOVE: *The Carte d'Identité of Violette Szabo, using the cover name Corinne Reine Leroy, which was used during her first mission in France. Many details were stated on identity cards, such as name, profession, date and place of birth, nationality and address. Physical features were also stated: height, eye and hair colour and the shape of the face. Violette Szabo's fingerprint is stamped on the bottom left-hand corner and on the top of the card, there is a stamp from the town hall which processed the document.*

ABOVE: *Typewriter used by SOE agent Tony Brooks, the organiser of PIMENTO, to counterfeit documents in France. Most of the forged documents were manufactured at the Thatched Barn.*

As well as being allocated false documents, each agent required a cover name which was printed on the forged documentation. This was a false name by which their neighbours and non-Resistance friends knew them. Yvonne Baseden recalled that she was given the name Madame Marie Bernier 'because this was easy and very common in France. There were many Berniers.'

As well as being given a cover name, the agents were also allocated a field name by which their Resistance colleagues would know them. Sometimes, if they were sent on a number of missions, they were given more than one codename. F section agent Lise de Baissac's codenames were 'Odile', 'Marguerite' and 'Irene'. Sometimes, carrying more than one set of identity documentation could lead to arrest. One agent was arrested when the name on his identity card did not match the name he gave. During a body search, two other false identity cards bearing different names were found on his person. He had given the card from the wrong pocket.

Agents were also allocated a cover story, giving them a profession. Male agents had to have an explanation as to why they were not in the Army, if they were of serviceable age. Many pretended to be in reserved occupations, such as travelling salesmen for firms producing war materials. F section tried to make the cover stories as real as possible and this often meant that they had some semblance of truth in them. Yvonne Baseden had been a short-hand typist in civilian life and her cover story stated that she was a secretary and Roger Landes, who had been a student in architecture, became Réné Pol, the architect. If questioned, their knowledge of their pre-war profession would augment their cover story.

Once they had been given their mission details, a cover story and some identity documents, the agents were ready to go. There were a number of ways of getting the agent into the field. The most popular was by air. The agents were sent to the holding schools, which were country houses near to the airfields from where they would take off. Tempsford in Bedfordshire was one of the airfields which F section used. In the hangar, known as Gibraltar Barn, they were searched for British coins, cigarettes and bus tickets. They were then allocated their L (lethal) pill – a small capsule of cyanide, which, when bitten in half, would release its poison. Some agents immediately discarded the pill in the belief that they wanted to survive no matter what happened to them. Others took the pill with them, knowing that they could not survive torture. One SOE agent, Gonzagues de St. Genies, codenamed 'Lucien', had already experienced German treatment as a POW and had informed Yvonne Baseden, his wireless operator, with whom he had parachuted into France, that he would take the capsule. When he faced arrest, having already sustained a head wound, he almost certainly did.

ABOVE: *Tempsford.*

ABOVE: *L (Lethal) pill which would enable the agent to commit suicide. This particular pill was carried by Douglas Dodds-Parker, the Commanding Officer of Massingham, in Algiers, North Africa, when flying over enemy territory.*

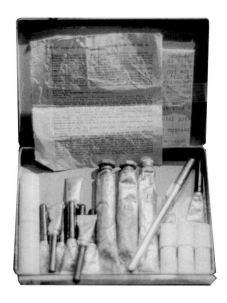

ABOVE: *First aid kit issued to Wing Commander Yeo-Thomas of RF section.*

Before leaving for France, every agent was presented with a gift from Colonel Maurice Buckmaster, the Head of F section. Yvonne Cormeau's silver powder compact is shown here. Women were given make-up compacts and cigarette cases, whilst men often received cuff links. Naturally, they didn't have 'Made in England' inscribed on them. Not only was this farewell gift a token of Buckmaster's esteem, it was also something which they could sell in order to raise funds.

In Gibraltar Barn at Tempsford airfield, they were allocated a substantial amount of French francs, Benzedrine tablets, which could be taken to combat tiredness, and some purification tablets, which, when dissolved, rendered stream water drinkable.

The agents were kitted out with their parachutes and jumping uniform, which was called the Striptease. This was because there were two zips on the front which could be undone from head to foot, enabling the agent to quickly step out of the garment upon landing. It was made of very thick, camouflaged canvas material which covered the shoes and went up to the neck. The agent wore a rubber helmet to protect the head. They were ready for the journey.

ABOVE: *SOE Jump suit: The Striptease. Note the two zips on the front to facilitate hasty undressing.*

The pilot located the dropping zone by a sequence of lights set by the reception committee. A pre-arranged letter would be flashed in Morse from the ground. If recognised, the pilot would alert the bods (RAF slang for agents) and the dispatcher would prepare them for jumping. If the pilot did not recognise the letter, he was not supposed to drop the bods as either he had the wrong field or was about to head into a trap.

The still (overleaf) is from the SOE film *Now It Can Be Told* and shows a dispatcher and real-life agent Jacqueline Nearne preparing to jump out of the aircraft. A set of lights in the back of the aeroplane prepared the agents for jumping. When the red light came on, the bods readied themselves by dangling their feet through the hole and when it turned to green, the dispatcher shouted 'Go!' and gently pushed the bod out. If they propelled themselves too far forward, they risked breaking their noses on the other side of the hole and this certainly happened to a number of agents.

The early agents were dropped blind, which meant that there was no reception committee to meet them, but as more agents were infiltrated, reception committees were organised to meet them. Some had pleasant surprises: RF agent, 19 year old Josiane Gros, was greeted by her mother who had landed by aircraft two months earlier; F section agent Pearl Witherington was met by her fiancé, Henri Cornioley. Some agents were not so lucky as they dropped to German controlled reception committees.

Madeleine Damerment was immediately arrested on landing and was executed at Dachau concentration camp in 1944.

When the agents landed, they were supposed to use a small shovel strapped to their calf to bury their silk parachute. Many agents however were instructed by members of the reception committee not to discard it because local women could use the silk fabric to make items of clothing, which were in short supply due to rationing.

Initially, SOE relied on RAF aircraft diverted from Bomber Command to fly their agents to France and no more than five were ever available. As the war progressed, RAF units were used solely for SOE operations. Special Duty Squadron No 138 was formed in August 1941 and flew from Tempsford in North London. In February 1942, No 161 was formed, operating from Tangmere in Sussex. By November 1942, 27 aircraft were at the disposal of SOE and 36 by spring 1944. The squadrons used Whitleys, Halifaxes, Stirlings and Lockheed Hudsons to parachute agents and supplies into France.

Parachuting agents into France was the most widely used method of entry. It had the advantage that 'bods' could be dropped within a reasonable distance of the area of operation. However, on many occasions, the pilot could not find the dropping ground or the signal letter was incorrect and they had to turn back. On Francis Cammaerts' second mission in France, bad weather caused the pilot to return. Approximately 250 miles from the intended dropping zone, the plane caught fire and Cammaerts had to bale out at 10,000 feet. It took him ten minutes to land.

There were only a few fatal parachute accidents including one which resulted from a bod not hooking up his static line which meant that the parachute was not connected to anything to open it. Another agent was mysteriously found dead on the ground despite no injuries and no signs of parachute failure. However, a number of agents had bad landings and many sustained injuries. Some landed in trees, on railway lines and on roofs. In June 1942, Bob Sheppard landed on a police roof in Burgundy and was captured immediately. Maureen O'Sullivan was dropped too low and fell on her back, but was protected by the 2,000,000 francs she had strapped on to her.

The main disadvantage with air operations was that everything depended on the moon. Agents could only be dropped during the moon period when there was enough light to guide the pilot. Bad weather also postponed journeys and one agent could not stand the pressure of constant deferments and left SOE.

As well as dropping missions, the Special Duty Squadrons carried out landing and pick-up operations using a single-engined monoplane. The Westland Lysander, nicknamed 'The Flying Carrot' because of its shape, was a small, light aeroplane which needed only a short take off and landing space of about 600 metres. Because of this, they were suitable for landing agents in France. They were adapted for agent pick-up duties by simply adding a long-range fuel tank between the wheels and a fixed ladder on the port side. There was usually only one crew member – the pilot – and the seat used by the machine gunner became available for the passenger.

Aircraft were guided down by a sequence of lights (hand-held torches) in an L shape. Following the exchange of pre-arranged Morse letters, the pilot would land his plane in the field using the lights as a guide . The length of the L shape would be the run in;

the pilot would then turn the Lysander around along the base of the L and be ready for take off once the exchange of agents and supplies had been accomplished.

The first Lysander mission to France occurred on 4 September 1941, when an agent was landed in a field near Issodun, south of Orleans. The aircraft spent two minutes on the ground before taking off with another passenger and returning to Britain. On one occasion, the pilot managed a record 12.5 second landing and take-off whilst under fire from German soldiers. During the war, Lysanders flew 279 operations. 102 agents were landed in France and 129 agents were collected from fields in France. Six pilots were killed.

Later in the war, the 'Rebecca-Eureka' was developed which was a radio homing device. A beacon pin-pointed the dropping ground enabling the approaching aircraft to land. The pilot was able to contact the reception committee on the ground and was guided in using the 'S-phone', which was a small portable radio telephone, which enababled the two to converse briefly. On one occasion, Maurice Buckmaster, head of F section, flew over in an aircraft and spoke to one of his very sucessful organisers George Starr using an S-phone.

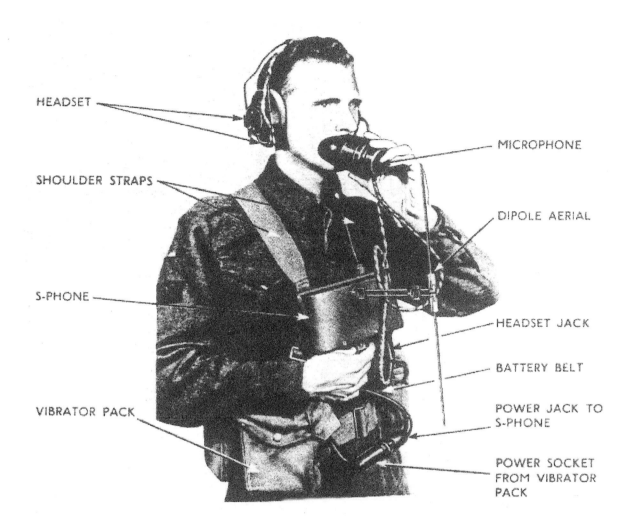

ABOVE: *An S-phone.*

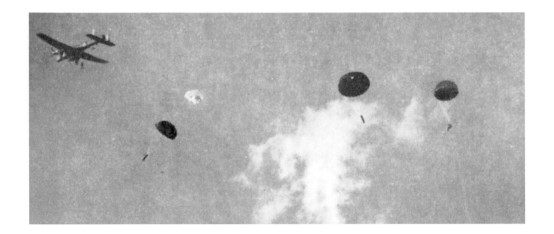

The first Hudson landing operation ocurred in February 1943. The Lockheed Hudson aircraft was a twin-engined bomber and unlike the Lysander was armed. It had a crew of four and could carry ten passangers, but as a result needed runways of about 1,000 metres to land and take off. The third aircraft which was used was the Douglas Dakota or DC3 with a crew of four. It could transport 20 passengers or two tons of freight.

As well as carrying agents, aircraft also dropped containers of arms. They had to be packed carefully at the base stations so as not to explode on impact. As well as a variety of weapons, such as Piats, Stens, Brens and hand grenades, containers also included clothing, money, wireless sets and food. Nancy Wake, an Australian woman who worked as a liaison officer in the

Auvergne district of France, received parcels marked 'Personal for Hélène' ('Hélène' was her code-name), which contained Elizabeth Arden make up products, as well as Brooke Bond tea, chocolates and confectionery. Quite often, the parachutes would be blown a few kilometres from the dropping zone and there was always a great hurry to locate and retrieve the containers. Many containers were either lost, claimed by rival resistance groups or picked up by German soldiers who had heard the planes overhead.

The 'C' type container dropped to the Resistance in France, consisted of an outer shell with three inner cells. The outer shell was hinged to allow cells to be lifted out. The containers were cylindrical, 5"8' in length, 15' in diameter and weighed 330lbs.

Although most frequently used, aircraft was not the only method of entry into France. Some agents were infiltrated by MTB (Motor Torpedo Boat) from the United Kingdom to the Brittany coast; others, such as Odette Sansom, were infiltrated by 'felucca' – Portuguese sardine trawlers – from Gibraltar to the Mediterranean coast. Unlike entry by air, sea journeys were not hampered by the moon period, but they were much slower and often took days to land the agents on the French coast.

CHAPTER 5

THE FANYs

Women in the British military services (the WAAF, the ATS and the WRNS) were precluded from combatant action by the Geneva Convention, which meant that SOE had to look elsewhere for a cover for its women recruits. In 1940, before he became the Executive Head of SOE, Colin Gubbins, the Director of Operations and Training, required some women to undertake confidential work. Phyllis Bingham, a family friend of Gubbins, informed him of the First Aid Nursing Yeomanry, of which she was the Commanding Officer's secretary. The FANYs provided SOE with the solution. Not only were they used to staff the coding and wireless stations, but the organisation also acted as a cover for the women agents who were put into FANY uniform.

LEFT: *Memorial plaque in Knightsbridge, Central London. The latin inscription reads 'in difficulties unconquered' which refers loosely to the FANY motto 'I Cope'.*

The FANYs were an independent, voluntary, women's service which was established in 1907 by Captain Edward Charles Baker. Whilst fighting in Kitchener's Sudan campaign in the 1890s, he noted that men needed immediate emergency treatment on the battlefields before being taken to a field hospital. He envisioned a women's organisation which could bridge the divide between the front line and the medical station. Women, trained in first aid, could ride side-saddle onto the battlefield to attend to the wounded. Having been given emergency treatment, the injured could then be transported by horse ambulance to the makeshift hospital behind the front line. After his return to Britain, Baker established the FANYs, which was the first women's service.

The FANY's voluntary status meant that they were not subject to military rules, such as the Geneva Convention, and thus they were an ideal organisation for SOE to utilise.

ABOVE: *Captain Baker and Lilian Franklin – who took over from Baker as the President or Patron of the FANYs from about 1911 – out riding in 1909, shortly after Franklin had joined.*

During the inter-war period, the FANYs changed their name to the Women's Transport Service (FANY) because it was considered that their role in the Great War, in which they drove ambulances, should be recognised. However, it never really took on and they were simply referred to as the FANYs.

The FANY uniform, which was khaki (shown right), was distributed during basic training at Overthorpe Hall, near Banbury, where new members were taught drill, Corp history and first aid and were expected to undertake a number of chores, such as blackleading grates.

The FANYs were sent on various courses to train to be coders and wireless operators. One such place was Fawley Court in Henley-on-Thames. Here, the wireless operators had to practice to

increase their transmitting speeds to about 25 words per minute and the coders learnt how to encode and decode. Once they had completed their training, they were posted to various base stations in England, North Africa, Italy and the Far East, where they worked alongside operators from the Royal Corps of Signals.

BELOW: *Wireless Operators stationed at Algiers, North Africa, in August 1944. Top row (left to right): Joan Tapp, Joan Olgilvie-Dalgleish, Diana Thatcher, Ann Bonsor, Margaret Ogilvy. Bottom row: Lorna Green, Peggy Thynne, Margaret Pratt, Marjorie Hobbs.*

ABOVE: *'The senior one, Marian, was rather stout, and the junior one, Hope, was rather thin, and they were always known colloquially to us as Fat Gamwell and Thin Gamwell.' (A FANY.) Marian, the Commander of the FANYs, is seated and her sister Hope, is standing on the left. On the right is Dorothy Hope-Morley.*

LEFT: *FANYs and Signalmen relaxing on the beach at Mount Lavinia, November 1945. (left to right) Derek Brundrett, Joyce Bethell, Betty Henderson, Philip Dawkins.*

BELOW: *FANYs and Signalmen in the Massingham Pantomime, Cinderella: The Story of a Downtrodden FANY, Algiers Christmas 1943.*

CHAPTER 6

CODES & SIGNALS

Codes and ciphers have been used since ancient times. The word cryptography means the science of codes and it derives from the Greek words Kryptos, meaning secret, and Graphos, meaning writing. Although often misconstrued as being the same thing, there are subtle differences between a code and cipher. A code is based on complete words or phrases and resembles a dictionary, in the sense that all the words are replaced by codewords or codenumbers. You need to possess a code book to send or read a code. A cipher, on the other hand, uses single letters. It is either jumbled up or replaced by other letters, numbers or symbols. Complicated ciphers incorporate both. This may be memorised and a code book is not necessary to either send or read a cipher.

LEFT: *This still, taken from the film, 'Now It Can be Told', shows real-life SOE agent, Jacqueline Nearne, as the fictional character Cat. Her finger is on the Morse key and she is sending a message to London.*

Each SOE agent had a personal code that was peculiar to them. An identical copy of this code was held at the base station so that when the messages came in from the field, they could be decoded. At the beginning of SOE activities, these codes were based on a single word or a series of numbers, known as a Playfair code, which guided the transposition. As SOE expanded, the coding became more complicated and was based on a well-known phrase or poem called a 'worked-out key' or a WOK. This system was refined by Leo Marks, the head of the Coding department of SOE's F section. He realised that popular poems could easily be recognised by the Germans who could then work out the whole code. For example, if the word 'Britannia' came out from the message, it could easily be deduced that the code was based on the line 'Rule Britannia, Britannia rules the waves'.

Leo Marks decided to replace the WOK with made-up poems. By writing their own poems, SOE could ensure that the Germans could never break their codes. The following poem was written by Leo Marks in memory of a girlfriend who died in a motorcycle crash and was given to Violette Szabo. It has become famous and is regarded as a symbol of F section.

The life that I have
Is all that I have
And the life that I have is yours.

The love that I have
Of the life that I have
Is yours and yours, and yours.

A sleep I shall have
A rest I shall have
Yet death will be but a pause.

For the peace of my years
In the long green grass
Will be yours and yours and yours.

Step 1:

When a message needed to be sent, the first task was to encode the message. One FANY coder remarked that 'each agent in the field had his or her paperback and the coding officer had an identical one. If you were encoding, you found any two consecutive lines on any page, you used the first five words in both and you wanted the letters in each line to add up to roughly 15 to 25.' For example:

THEYCAME BACKTOTHE

WEVEGOTTOWORKTOMORROW

Step 2:

Number the letters in the first grid in alphabetical order. If 2 letters are the same, number that which appears first, one, then the next one, two.

T	H	E	Y	C	A	M	E	B	A	C	K	T	O	T	H	E
14	9	6	17	4	1	12	7	3	2	5	11	15	13	16	10	8

Step 3:

Write the message horizontally underneath the 5 word quote to form a cage. It must not be a perfect quadrilateral. If that occurs, then add a few extra XXXs.

T	H	E	Y	C	A	M	E	B	A	C	K	T	O	T	H	E
14	9	6	17	4	1	12	7	3	2	5	11	15	13	16	10	8
C	O	M	E	H	O	M	E	A	T	O	N	C	E	S	T	O
P	W	I	L	L	S	E	N	D	P	L	A	N	E	T	U	E
S	D	A	Y	N	I	N	T	H	S	T	O	P	U	S	U	A
L	P	L	A	C	E											

Step 4:

Write out the second line, numbering the letters as they occur.

W	E	V	E	G	O	T	T	O	W	O	R	K	T	O	M	O	R	R	O	W
19	1	18	2	3	6	15	16	7	20	8	12	4	17	9	5	10	13	14	11	21

Step 5:

Start at column one of grid one (shown in step 3) and read vertically. Transfer letters into grid 2 horizontally. So, for example, the first four letters in our new grid would be O S I E, followed by T P S from column 2.

W	E	V	E	G	O	T	T	O	W	O	R	K	T	O	M	O	R	R	O	W
19	1	18	2	3	6	15	16	7	20	8	12	4	17	9	5	10	13	14	11	21
O	S	I	E	T	P	S	A	D	H	H	L	N	C	O	L	T	M	I	A	L
E	N	T	O	E	A	O	W	D	P	T	U	U	N	A	O	M	E	N	E	E
U	C	P	S	L	C	N	P	S	T	S	E	L	Y	A						

Step 6:

Reading vertically, starting at column 1, transpose letters onto a pad which will then be transmitted in groups of 5 by the wireless operator. The code must be labelled so that the receiver knows where the quote is in the book. For example, 02716 means page 27, line 16.

02716   SNCEO   STELN   ULLOP   ACDDS   HTSOA
ATMAE   LUEME   INSON   AWPCN   YITPO   EUHPT   LI

Once the message had been sent from the field and taken down by the wireless operators at the base stations, it then had to be decoded. Members of the FANY mainly undertook this task.

For decoding, the operator writes out the second line first, then makes a cage of the 57 letters and decodes by filling in vertically and then transposing in the first cage horizontally.

Sometimes the messages were unreadable and these were called indecipherables. One FANY explained that 'these were messages which came out as complete gibberish or else partially came out with combinations that looked like some of the letters of proper words. The latter were the most interesting to try and solve. The agent (in France or the Low Countries) was operating under great pressure and it was easy to make a mistake. There were a number of ways he could go wrong and the trick was to find out what he had done. It was a great challenge, especially as time was so often important.' The FANYs would attack these indecipherables over and over again, sometimes using about 30,000 combinations to try to figure out where the error was.

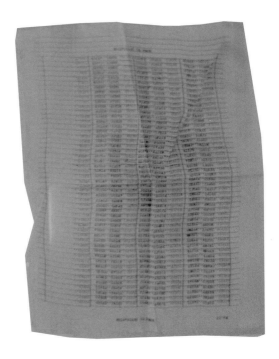

ABOVE: *Silk code sheet.*

One Time Pads (OTP) replaced the Worked Out Key (WOK). Each F section agent was issued with a pad of silk slips upon which were printed rows of letters and figures. This system devised by Leo Marks was called the One Time Pad because they were used only once and then burnt. This meant that the system was much more secure because the Gestapo could not read the back traffic if the code had been burnt. This also cut down on the length of time that agents were on the air. Some FANYs regretted the change to One Time Pads, although they recognised that it was better for the agents, because, as one coder remarked, 'sadly, there were no more indecipherables'.

The One Time Pads worked in a different way to the Worked Out Key. Both the agent and the coding office had identical pads which were pages of randomly selected groups of 5 letters. The first group was transmitted in clear which told the receiver where to start. The encoder then wrote out the message under the letters of the pad. So for example;

P R A M B   A H U R V   I Q S T U   F A R D P
            C O M E H   O M E A T   O N C E S

H L I M B   Z T R A M
T O P W I   L L S E N

By consulting the crib, which was a sheet of cardboard with all the letters of the alphabet on it, written in columns, you could unravel the code. For example:

AA = M

AB = T

AC = V

AD = P

You then wrote out the answer in groups of five letters. So the first one, AC would be V and because AC = V, then AV = C. For the purpose of decoding, the agent would write the message beneath letters in the pad. Therefore A over V would become C. Unlike the WOK code, this was unbreakable because the actual letters of the message were not incorporated.

Although there were no more indecipherables, there was still the challenge of speed. One could learn the combinations on the key card by word association and thus not have to look at the code book. One FANY remembered that 'if AB = T, you thought AB? and ABATE sprang to mind. With AT you thought AT? And if nothing came to mind, you thought A?T and then again you got ABATE. Some combinations were impossible and had to be remembered cold, but if you were de-coding, a good operator could eventually hold the message in her left hand under the appropriate group on the pad, and write the answer out with her right hand without referring to the crib. You probably got a few letters wrong. That was easily rectified when you translated the groups of five letters into their proper words. To this day, if I'm following a car, I often try a word association with its number!' Each agent was allocated a number of security checks which, if correctly used, indicated that the agents were transmitting freely, and if incorrectly used meant that the agents were operating under duress. These checks might include a deliberate error, such as transposing the letters P and R, always getting the eighth letter of a message wrong or replacing every thirteenth letter with the one preceding it in the alphabet. Through the use of torture, the Gestapo became aware of the existence of these checks. In order to combat this, F section gave their agents a bluff check which they could reveal to the Germans if captured. If this appeared in the text, the home station would know that the agent had been arrested.

However, once in the field, not everything worked out so smoothly. Enemy jamming made it difficult to hear the Morse and mistakes in the coding made it difficult to determine whether the mistakes were deliberate or accidental. By the time the decoded message arrived on the desk of the country section's staff, it had been encoded, transmitted, received, decoded and teleprinted. Each could have brought with it errors, although the most likely was at the initial stage. It was not always so easy to remember how to use these security checks properly once in the field, because of the pressures of mounting communications and increased arrests. Some agents forgot to incorporate their true security check or put it in the wrong place. Worse still was when captured agents followed correct procedure by omitting their true security check and incorporating their bluff check, but were reminded by home station, who assumed it to be a mistake, not to leave out their true check. Gilbert Norman (code name 'Archambault') experienced this when he was captured. After sending a message, omitting his true security check and incorporating only his bluff check, he received a reply reminding him of the importance of using security checks. Maurice Southgate, on returning from Buchenwald concentration camp, remarked that he met a number of victims of this error and reported 'time after time, for different men, London sent back messages saying "my dear fellow, you only left us a week ago. On your first message you go and forget to put your true check." (S/Ldr Southgate would very much like to know what the hell the check was meant for if not for that very special occasion.)'

The basic criteria for military wireless sets was that they had to operate a number of interference-free channels, had to have a good range, be robust, easy to operate, simple to maintain and portable. These factors were often incompatible. Thus a set which was produced to have a wide range, was often bulky, difficult to conceal and needed a well-spread-out aerial, which as a result could be easily spotted. However, throughout the course of the war, the British electronics industry made steady improvements to wireless equipment. Sets were produced that were lighter, more reliable, with an increased range and reduced power needs.

Initially, SOE did not have its own independent signals section; it had to secure a wavelength allotment from an inter-service frequency and equipment was supplied by it's rival, SIS (Secret Intelligence Service). Eventually, in June 1942, it was agreed that SOE should control its own wireless communications, design and build its own sets, train its own operators, invent its own ciphers and do its own deciphering. SOE's own design team produced a series of suitcase sets, beginning with the A Mark I (or Type 3 MKI) in August 1942. This first attempt by SOE to build its own set, used obsolete, bulky, fragile tubes which contributed to its total weight of 42 pounds. The set had a range of 500 miles and only used CW transmission. It was quickly replaced by the A Mark II in October 1942 and the B2 (or Type 3 MKII) in 1943. The B2 set was especially perfected for clandestinity, weighing only

30 pounds and was easily concealed inside a small suitcase. But because of its size, it had a weak signal producing no more than 20 watts. It had a wide frequency range, from 3.5 to 16 megacycles a second, but because of this, it needed over 70 feet of aerial. Its superheterodyne receiver was highly selective and effectively rejected interfering signals. This was the set most widely used by operators in France.

A member of the Royal Corps of Signals recalled that 'the B Mark II set, which was installed in a suitcase, was used by the secret agents operating in enemy occupied territories. The BII set was quite different from any set I had so far employed. Its use was solely for W/T, and we worked on VHF, Very High Frequencies, which gave the best possible reception conditions. The frequencies we used we selected by the means of crystals which were plugged into the set.' Most of the sets were installed in suitcases so they could be carried around by the wireless operator or courier when they found new places from which to transmit. However, if the agent was stopped and the suitcase was opened, it was obvious that it was a radio set. To combat this, SOE's camouflage section tried to disguise some sets as other objects, such as sewing machines.

BELOW: *The B2 (or Type 3, Mark II) suitcase transceiver which was the most widely used set in France. It was powered by either mains or battery and had a range of over 1,000 miles.*

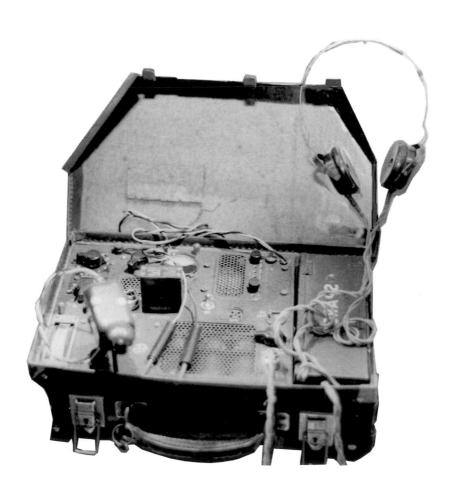

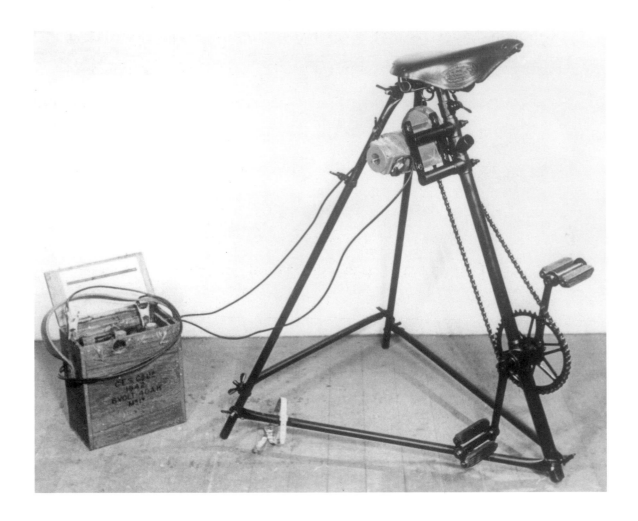

ABOVE: *A peddle-operated battery-charger in the operating position. Instead of working off the mains, some sets required manpower to make them work. Resisters would have taken it in turns to peddle as fast as possible to generate enough power to charge the battery to enable the operator to transmit their message.*

Although the sets used by SOE were modified during the war, they basically operated in the same way. The radio was assembled in four parts: a receiver, a transmitter, a long aerial and a crystal. The crystal, which would enable the agent to operate on a certain pre-arranged frequency when inserted into the set, was difficult to disguise. If found on them, they were very difficult to explain away as they bore no resemblance to anything else. However, because of their small size, they could be readily concealed. Nevertheless, they were very easily broken as they were delicate and were difficult to replace. The set then had to be plugged into the mains electricity current or attached to a car battery or other source of power. However, the use of the mains electricity supply was dangerous. The German intelligence service could trace an unauthorised transmission in about 20 minutes by using three different detectors and closing in on the target. They used direction-finding (D/F) equipment to track clandestine wireless communications. They would cut off the supply of electricity by sub-district, and note when the transmission was interrupted, to narrow down the focus of their efforts. Then a Gestapo agent holding a miniature listening set to his ear, with his collar turned up and the brim of his hat pulled down obscuring his face, would be used. The strength of the pulse increased as the Gestapo agent got nearer to the building from which the signal was being transmitted, enabling them to pinpoint the location. Alternatively, they could employ D/F vans which contained a small listening station. The wireless operators could prevent detection if they changed the crystals which altered the frequencies, during the transmission. Then the Gestapo would have to restart their search, having lost the signal.

ABOVE: *Crystals which were plugged into the wireless set to change the frequency.*

The wireless operators were given a schedule when they could come on air, called a 'Sked'. This was when they were expected to contact the home station. Even if they had nothing to report, they were expected to come up on air and give the signal QRU – I have no message for you. This was part of the 'Q' Code: a commercial code used by SOE to cut down on the length of time the operators were on air. The signals were in groups of three letters. For example: QTC meant I have a message for you; QRV meant message received and QSA, followed by a number from one to five, indicated the strength of the signal. QSA 1, for example, meant that the agent was receiving a very weak, almost inaudible, message, whereas QSA 5 was very clear.

Another signal was added to the Q code: QUG. This meant "breaking off transmission. I am in imminent danger." Many of the FANY W/T operators in the base stations recalled receiving one of these signals. One FANY wireless operator recalled 'once I received QUG which meant: "I am in imminent danger, close down." We then listened for all subsequent schedules and were overjoyed when weeks later he came up and we knew he was safe. Obviously we were all very concerned for the safety of agents, but

I think the fact that we did not know them personally helped us not to be emotionally involved, when we knew they might be in danger. We were just anxious to be sure of picking them up if and when they were in a position to transmit again.'

The agent would key in their message using a code and a FANY or a Royal Corps of Signals Sergeant would listen, writing down the Morse. The agent was supposed to keep the messages short, since direction-finding (DF) vans could pick up a signal within 20 minutes. However, many messages were very long and they remained on the air for a dangerously long time. A number of agents were arrested at their sets because they stayed on too long. The personnel at the base stations had to try to ensure that they wrote down the message accurately, without asking the agent to repeat a section since this greatly increased the likelihood of arrest.

Often the enemy jammed the messages which sometimes made the signal inaudible. This, coupled with the mistakes made by the agents in the field who were under enormous pressure, meant that messages were often garbled and took the coders many hours to unravel. Because of the speed at which the agents were transmitting, the operators at the home stations had to devise ways of taking down the previous letter, whilst listening to the next. One FANY remembered perfecting her technique: 'because we could not write in running hand, and capital letters take longer, one learnt by a knack to be writing two letters behind the one you were actually hearing-which meant memorising two letters other than the one you were writing and to write them down in proper sequence. I trained for four months for this!'

Each operator is said to have a unique style which is distinctive to them, like hand-writing. This was called a fist. Before wireless operators left for the field, their sending style was recorded. The fingerprinting section, headed by a Miss Cameron, was responsible for doing this. The characteristics of the operator were recorded on tape and trained personnel could detect whether or not the person operating the wireless set in the field was the agent. This was known as the 'Tina' system.

Wireless traffic was received at Grendon Underwood, now an open prison, which was staffed by FANY operators and Signalmen. The signals room had 18 operating positions, each equipped with a wireless set and sheets of squared paper on which to write down the coded messages. There was also a superintendent's desk which enabled them to listen in to any of the sets.

In 1942, Grendon, Station 53A, was the only receiver site in Britain. Due to ever-increasing wireless traffic, another station had to be built. Poundon, Station 53B, was much larger and had 40 operating positions.

RIGHT: *FANYs operating their sets at a base station. Note the numbers on each position and the poster 'Remember The Enemy Is Listening'.*

CHAPTER 7

GADGETS & WEAPONS

SOE's Directorate of Scientific Research invented numerous specialised devices which were employed by its agents in the various theatres of war: silenced firearms, concealed weapons, hidden compasses, camouflaged explosives. The Directorate, under DM Newitt, was based at Station IX, The Frythe, in a requisitioned Welwyn Garden City hotel. Many of the devices developed here assumed the prefix Wel to denote their location. The Welrod, a firearm with a silencer, and the Welbike, a portable and foldable bicycle are just two examples.

LEFT: *Sub-Lieutenant Jimmy Holmes RNVR testing out the Welman One-Man submarine on Loleham reservoir in Staines.*

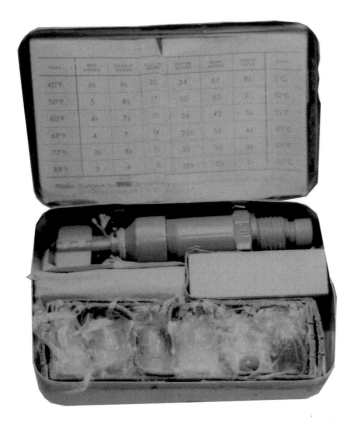

ABOVE LEFT: *AC delay set. The concentration of acid in the glass phials delayed the detonation of the limpet mine from anything between four hours to five days.*

ABOVE RIGHT: *Anti-disturbance fuse for the limpet mine. Any attempt to remove a limpet with this fuse in place would result in the detonation of the mine.*

OVERLEAF: *Testing the 'Sleeping Beauty', a motorised submersible canoe or MSC, at St. Albans. Note the breathing apparatus.*

BELOW: *Sleeping Beauty explosive charge with magnetic attachment and buoyancy bag.*

ABOVE LEFT: *The Welmine, designed at Station IX in Welwyn Garden City. It was an anti-shipping mine which sunk to a pre-determined depth. A number of the Station IX devices were not manufactured and the Welmine was neither put into production, nor used operationally.*

ABOVE RIGHT: *Limpet mine concealed in a Shell petrol can. This type of mine was used by SOE saboteurs against enemy shipping.*

ABOVE: *Limpet mine Type 6 Mark II with AC delay fuse. Contained two pounds of plastic explosive.*

From June 1942, Station IX had a subsection called the Thatched Barn. It had been used by employees and visitors to the film studio at the nearby Elstree studios. The boss of the Thatched Barn, Major J Elder Wills, later Lt Col, had also been in the film industry before the war. He was one of several SOE section heads from whom Ian Fleming developed his character Q, played by Desmond Llewellyn, for the Bond movies.

The Thatched Barn was demolished in 1990 to make way for the Elstree Moat House but during the war, the 'dirty tricks' department was responsible for exploding rats, animal-dung tyrebursters and explosive coal.

The explosive coal was made in two halves in moulds with the explosive put in. The two halves of plaster and papier-mâché would then be sealed around the explosive. When the fake coal was tossed into furnaces or trains' boilers, it would explode creating havoc. Exploding rats had the same effect. An incision was made in a dead rat. The skin was cured. Then the rat was filled with plastic explosive and stitched up. When thrown into a factory furnace, the rat would explode causing much damage and a delay to the factory's production. This simple ruse was particularly effective. When the Germans cottoned onto it, every rat was inspected before being thrown in to the furnace, which was time-consuming, as well as extremely unpleasant. It is claimed that nine Belgian factory boilers were put out of action by rat bombs.

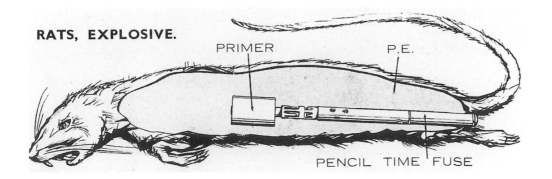

RATS, EXPLOSIVE.

PRIMER   P.E.

PENCIL TIME FUSE

Underneath the diagram of the 'rat' in the 'Descriptive Catalogue of Special Devices and Supplies' is the following description:

'A rat is skinned, the skin being sewn up and filled with a PE to assume the shape of a dead rat. A Standard No 6 Primer is set in the PE. Initiation is by means of a short length of safety fuse with a No 27 detonator crimped on one end, and a copper tube ignited on the other end, or, as in the case of the illustration above, a PTF with a No 27 detonator attached. The rat is then left amongst the coal beside a boiler and the flames initiate the safety fuze when the rat is thrown on to the fire, or as in the case of the P.T.F. a Time Delay is used.'

The artificial animal-dung tyrebursters were also made in moulds and resembled the animals found in the country into which they were to be dropped. Manure arrived from London Zoo and was studied for texture, colour and shape. Explosive camel, elephant, donkey, sheep and horse manure were all developed at the Thatched Barn. These 'tyrebursters' were strategically placed by members of the Resistance on roads. This was especially useful following D-Day. The French Resistance were able to delay columns of German vehicles attempting to travel north to bolster their Divisions. German soldiers had to spend many painstaking hours checking whether the animal droppings in the road were artificial or real and their pace was greatly slowed. In total, 185,813 explosive tyrebursters in 150 different varieties of stones, rocks, mud, bricks and droppings were produced at the Thatched Barn. Each of these devices could be ordered from the 'Descriptive Catalogue of Special Devices and Supplies'.

Other devices developed at the Thatched Barn included rubber soles, below, which were attached to the underside of agents' boots. These were designed for the sand and jungle soil of the Far East. Instead of leaving the boot print of an agent, which would inform the enemy of a landing, the shoe left an impression of a bare footprint.

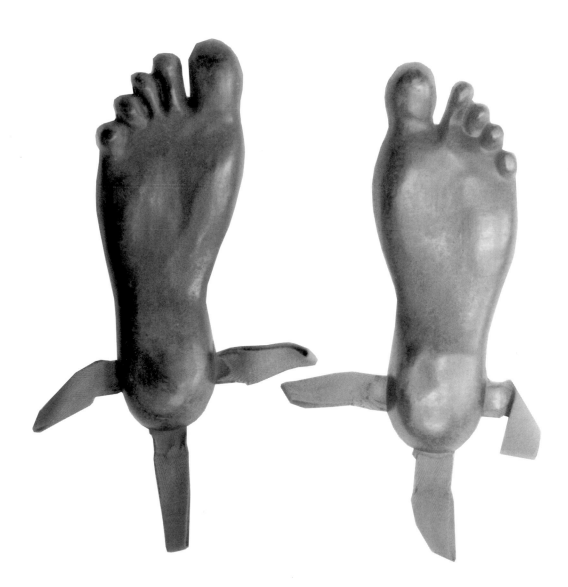

The Thatched Barn also developed explosive bicycle pumps, which worked normally until the safety catch was removed and pumping began, incendiary cigarettes, explosive Dutch clogs, artificial logs for concealing weapons, explosive torches, Chianti bottles fitted as time bombs and wireless transmitters disguised as vacuum cleaners, sewing machines and musical instruments.

BELOW: *Picture of fountain pen – issued to SOE agent Tony Brooks to conceal micro-photographs of his D-Day messages.*

ABOVE: *Dagger concealed in a pencil.*

SOE provided its agents with a number of intriguing gadgets which were later to inspire 007 creator, Ian Fleming. One such device invented by SOE researchers resembled a fountain pen but instead of using ink, it fired tear-gas. When disabled, the pen worked normally, but when it was primed, tear gas would be emitted from the lid. The tear gas firing pen used a .38 calibre tear-gas cartridge and could be employed at short-range. By injecting the tear gas into the air, it gave the agent a few seconds to escape. Wing Commander Yeo-Thomas, who worked for RF section, was carrying this gadget in his pocket when he was captured. He was seized by five men in civilian clothes who immediately handcuffed his hands behind his back making it impossible for him to reach his tear-gas pen.

ABOVE: *Tear gas pen. This fired a .38 calibre ampoule of tear gas, sufficient to incapacitate an aggressor and enable an agent to make their escape.*

TOP: *Knuckle-duster used by SOE agents. Four fingers are inserted into the holes and when the agent punched the opponent, it was steel, not flesh, which hit them.*

BELOW: *A Fairbairn-Sykes double-edged commando knife with eight-inch blade. This particular knife was issued to Jedburgh Jim Menzies, member of Team JULIAN.*

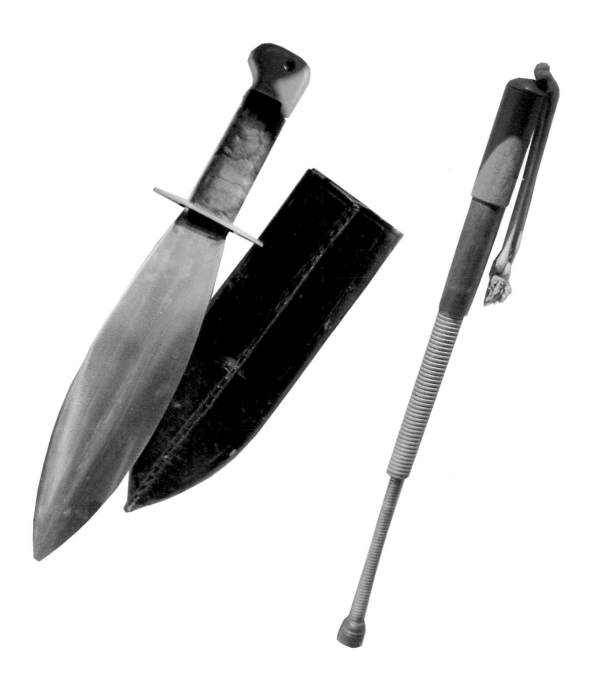

ABOVE LEFT: *Fairbairn-Sykes fighting knive and scabbard. The knife is a Smatchet. It was a fighting knife designed as both a stabbing and a slashing weapon.*

ABOVE RIGHT: *Spring-loaded cosh.*

Agents were equipped with coshes, knuckle-dusters and commando knives to protect themselves if they chose. Captains Fairbairn and Sykes were two Shanghai policemen who were drafted into SOE to train agents in unarmed combat and silent killing. They invented the double-edged commando knife and Fairbairn wrote a manual called 'All-in Fighting' which depicted the uses of the commando knife.

Plastic Explosive (PE) had been developed just before the outbreak of war in the Royal Arsenal at Woolwich. It was useful for SOE because it could be cut and shaped easily. SOE also used other explosives, Ammonal, Gelignite and Dynamite, but PE was the most effective. In order to delay the detonation of the explosive charges, a time switch was developed, known as Switch No 9 or L Delay. A lead element under a spring tension would break at a set time and a striker fired the detonator to which the delay was attached. Later in the war, SOE researchers manufactured their own delay switch called the Time Pencil or Switch No 10. Contact between corrosive liquid and a piece of wire which retained the striker, detonated the Time Pencil. They were issued ready-timed, ranging from minutes to hours. Over 12 million Time Pencils were produced. One disadvantage to the delay switches was that they were affected by temperature which changed the detonation time. SOE agent Ben Cowburn, the organiser of the TINKER circuit, used time pencils with a two hour delay on the night of 3/4 July 1943 to derail train engines at Troyes. After only 30 minutes, the detonations began.

A further device which was developed by SOE researchers was abrasive grease which was filled with ground carborundum. It was supplied in realistic-looking cans and was used on vehicle axle-bearings. It proved very successful in Tony Brook's PIMENTO circuit. On 7 June 1944, two girls aged 16 and 14, applied the abrasive grease to the axles of rail-cars transporting tanks. Every one of them seized up and as a result, the 2nd SS Panzer Division's tanks were delayed for over a fortnight.

ABOVE LEFT: *Time pencils (or Switch No 10) which were used to detonate explosives.*

ABOVE RIGHT: *Fog signal igniter. SOE developed this gadget, which, in peacetime, was employed to warn railway engineers of fog on the line, and converted it into a detonating device.*

ABOVE: *Standard charge with attached fuses and detonators. This particular charge contains one and half pounds of plastic explosive.*

SOE researchers invested much time and money in experimenting with silenced weapons. In the same way that shooting through a pillow controls the speed of the volume of air coming out and reduces the noise of the bullet, the silenced weapon is relatively quiet because of the velocity and the constrained space for air. Gasses, which were released by pulling the trigger, were bled off into the baffles or rubber rings inside the barrel, which reduced the noise level from supersonic to subsonic levels. This had the advantage of preventing the crack made by a supersonic bullet in flight. In 1943, Station IX manufactured the Welrod, which was a repeating pistol. In other words, the bullets were loaded by magazine but needed to be manually re-loaded and re-cocked after each shot. It was produced in 7.65mm calibres, which verged on supersonic, and in 9mm calibres, which was more popular because of its size.

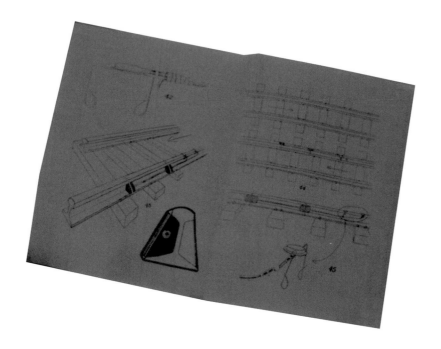

ABOVE: *Instructional booklets, such as this one on how to set an explosive charge on a railway line, accompanied containers of arms and ammunition, and were parachuted to resistance groups. This particular leaflet is in six languages.*

ABOVE: *A 9mm silenced Welrod, nicknamed the 'bicycle pump', designed at The Frythe.*

ABOVE: *Polish 9mm Radom automatic pistol. This gun was issued to SOE agent Christine Granville, the Polish heiress who saved the life of her JOCKEY organiser, Francis Cammaerts.*

ABOVE: *A Mark II 9mm Sten submachine-gun.*

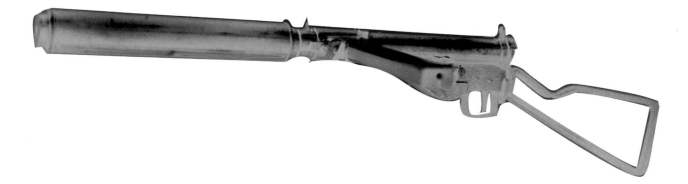

ABOVE: *A Mark II 9mm Sten submachine-gun with fitted silencer.*

The silencer was developed by SOE scientists.

ABOVE: *General-purpose grenade which could be used either as a*

hand grenade or as an explosive charge.

One of the weapons that was most utilised by the SOE was the Sten gun (or Machine-Carbine) which had been developed by the Royal Arms Factory in response to the need for automatic firepower, over 200,000 of which went to France. The advantage of the Sten gun was that it could be broken into four parts (magazine, barrel, body and butt), it could be easily assembled and it could be concealed. 32 bullets were held in the magazine, which jutted out at right angles to the barrel and it was particularly suited to right-handed people. It had a range of about 150 metres, but was at its best at 50 or 75 metres. This was because the disadvantage of the Sten gun was that it occasionally jammed. The assassination of Heydrich, a high-ranking Nazi Officer in Czechoslavakia, was hampered by Josef Gabčik's Sten gun failing to fire, which resulted in hand grenades having to be thrown. One agent operating in Sumatra dropped the Sten gun and it went off, killing him.

TOP: *Gammon grenade which was filled with plastic explosive. This was used to explode vehicles.*

BOTTOM: *Tyresule incendiary device which was filled with paraffin.*

ABOVE: *A Swiss Luger 7.65mm automatic pistol belonging to SOE agent Tony Brooks. It was given to him by a member of his PIMENTO circuit in Lyons but he did not carry it on him. Brooks believed it was safer not to have a weapon in case he was searched.*

ABOVE: *Thumb knife that could be concealed within clothing and remain undetected during a search. The handle of the knife is ridged so that the thumb doesn't slip in combat.*

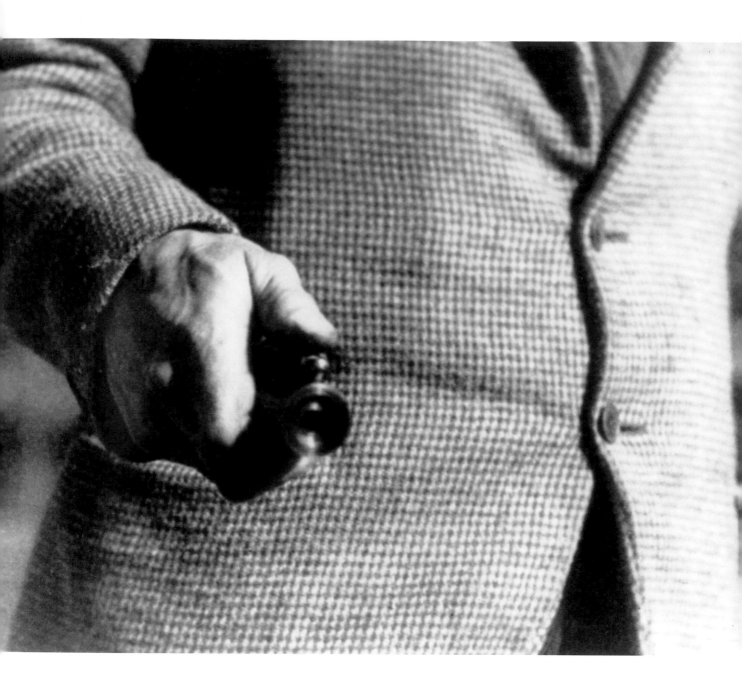

ABOVE: *This small gun, which fired only one bullet, was developed at the Frythe, and was a last resort upon capture.*

ABOVE: *Smith & Wesson .38 revolver used by SOE agents.*

CHAPTER 8

THE MAQUIS

Following the labour laws of 1943, a scheme was initiated which made it compulsory for men aged between 20 and 23 to be directed into work in Germany. Many fled to the countryside in order to avoid the call up. This compulsory work service, called the STO (service du travail obligatoire) boosted the ranks of the Maquis, a guerrilla-like organisation which lived on hillsides and in forests. The word Maquis (pronounced ma-key) is Corsican in origin, meaning 'scrub' or 'bush' in French and refers to the thick undergrowth which envelops the island. The definition points to the location of the Maquis; it was numerically stronger in the rural south and made use of the mountainous territory native to this region. Members of the Maquis, called maquisards, were mainly derived from the peasantry. They formed small

LEFT: *Maquisards studying a map before an operation. The man on the right is likely to be the organiser or leader of the maquisards and he is wearing a brassard with the Croix de Lorraine (Cross of Lorraine), the symbol of Free France, stitched on it.*

bands, were almost exclusively male and were very loosely organised. They built camps in forest clearings and on plateaux on hillsides. They lived in log cabins they built for themselves or in quickly constructed tents to shield them from the weather. As well as living off the land, they also relied on farmers' hospitality to provide food for them.

The Maquis specialised in sabotage and ambushing German troops. SOE armed the Maquis and often sent in weapons instructors to personally train maquisards. A number of F section agents worked with the maquis, including Nancy Wake, Yvonne Cormeau and Francis Cammaerts.

ABOVE: *Many of the maquisards wore armbands such as the above. FFI stood for Forces Françaises d'Intérieur (French Forces of the Interior). The name underneath was the area in which the Maquis operated and from which they got their name. For example, Maquis Bourgogne.*

The FFI was established in March 1944 by de Gaulle and functioned as an umbrella organisation which brought together the Maquis and the numerous ideologically-distant clandestine networks. By uniting these disparate groups under de Gaulle's authority, resistance was being reclaimed as a French-controlled activity, rather than being regarded as under the auspices of Britain. In his Mémoires, de Gaulle states 'local clandestine activities had to take on at the right moment the character of a national effort; had to become consistent enough to play a part in allied strategy; and, lastly, had to lead the army of the shadows to fuse with the rest into a single French army.'

OVERLEAF: *The Maquis of Limousin are captured on film whilst some relax and others are in cookhouse fatigues.*

CHAPTER 9

SABOTAGE

SOE agents were responsible for undertaking sabotage acts throughout France. Factories producing wartime materials were principal targets for resistance circuits. Hydro-electric power stations, local mines and the motor and aircraft industries were all attacked. The rubber industry was also targeted and in particular, the Dunlop factory in Montlucon and the Micheline factory at Clermont-Ferrand were put out of action. Brian Rafferty, organiser of STATIONER circuit, planned an attack on the Michelin works at Clermont-Ferrand in June 1943. The Peugeot motor works at Sochaux near the Swiss border, which had been classified as the third most important industrial target in France, was sabotaged in November 1943. Bomber Command

LEFT: *Resistance worker standing beside a derailed railway engine following sabotage on the Grenoble-Marseilles line in which he took part.*

had spent months trying to put this factory out of action and SOE agents with the help of local resistance workers accomplished it in a matter of minutes without any civilian casualties. As well as Peugeot and Michelin, SOE and the French Resistance put out of action a total of 90 factories.

Railways were another target. Between June 1943 and May 1944, 1,822 locomotives and 8,000 goods trucks were damaged by sabotage. As D-Day neared, the attacks intensified and a co-ordinated plan to halt all rail traffic was employed.

Each circuit was given a sentence that they had to listen out for on the BBC Messagés Personnel which would inform them that D-Day was approaching. The BBC's personal messages were broadcast between 7.30pm and 9pm. Families and Resistance workers would crowd around their radios to listen to these messages, despite the fact that tuning into the BBC was illegal and punishable by deportation. The messages were preceded by the first four notes of Beethoven's Fifth Symphony which was the V for Victory signal in Morse. The notes were followed by the sentence 'Voici quelques messages personnels.' ('Here are some personal messages.') The BBC announcer would read the messages twice in French, first at normal speed and then at a slower speed. These messages were usually nonsense, such as 'La chat est rouge' ('The cat is red') but they would alert a particular network to the arrival of a new agent, an arms drop or the imminence of D-Day, and because nothing in the text hinted at the meaning of the message, they were unbreakable. To the resistance group who had foreknowledge of this message, it meant a great deal.

On the evening of 5 June 1944, the Action messages were heard throughout France. Upon hearing their message, the group would begin blowing up petrol dumps, sabotaging local railway lines, blowing up bridges and setting up barricades on main roads, in order to hinder and delay German troop movement towards the Normandy bridgehead. Without the actions of the Resistance, there would have been many more German divisions converging on Normandy.

There are very few photographs of the havoc that resisters caused. Francis Cammaerts, an F section agent, noted 'we didn't go around with cameras after we'd blown something up!' However, there are some examples shown on the following pages.

OVERLEAF: *Bridge over the River Guil at Embrun, in the Haute Savoie, destroyed by the Resistance in August 1944. As a result of its collapse, German troops could not cross the river and were marooned in Embrun. They had to find alternative means of crossing and were significantly delayed.*

RIGHT: *A member of the French Resistance setting an explosive charge on a railway line in Roanne station. He only had three weeks training and wanted his photograph taken whilst setting the device to prove to his instructors that he was following procedures correctly. He even painted the charges white so that they would show up in the photograph.*

RIGHT AND OVERLEAF: *It wasn't just the French Resistance who participated in railway sabotage. The Belgians also inflicted damage on the German war effort as these pictures testify. They capture the mayhem resulting from the sabotage of a train carrying German troops. Members of the Belgian Partisan Army had set explosives on the Louvain-Ottignies line at Old-Heverlee on the 30 September 1943. The train had derailed, causing the destruction of the convoy and the death of 285 Germans.*

FOLLOWING PAGE: *Derailment wasn't the only sabotage that the Maquis engaged in. The photograph displays a German aeroplane which has been destroyed by the Maquis at Jumeau le Grand on 10 June 1944. The swastika is clearly visible on the tail of the aircraft and the propeller and most of the front of the plane has been damaged. It is likely that the plane crash-landed or was shot down and the damage was inflicted to the machine by the Maquis afterwards.*

CHAPTER 10

SUPPRESSION

On 18 October 1942, Hitler asserted that the Special Forces were comprised of criminals trained to kill with bare hands. A circular was issued which ordered the extermination of its members, regardless of whether or not they were in uniform or unarmed.

Heinrich Himmler, left, the head of the SS (SchutzStaffel) and Chief of the German Police, stated:

> 'The agents should die, certainly, but not before torture, indignity and interrogation has drained from them the last shred of evidence that should lead us to others. Then, and only then, should the blessed release of death be granted to them.'

The Abwehr, meaning 'Defence' in English, was a military Intelligence organisation which was established on 21 January 1921. An army of 100,000 men was permitted to Germany under the Treaty of Versailles purely for defensive purposes and an Abwehr section was formed in the German Ministry of Defence in Berlin under Colonel Gempp. As the Nazis took over control of Germany, it grew in size, peaking at about 15,000 people. Wilhelm Canaris assumed control on 1 January 1935 and its function expanded to incorporate offensive intelligence work in Germany and abroad.

Its overall remit was to protect the troops and to prevent acts of sabotage against the Wehrmacht. Its role of counteracting foreign intelligence services brought it into contact with resistance organisations and although it is the Gestapo which is renowned for incarcerating resistance workers, the Abwehr was also involved. The Abwehr was separate to the Gestapo and has often been compared to it in a more favourable light. Being turned over to the Gestapo was often used as a threat to induce agents to reveal names of other resistance members, their codes or the whereabouts of arms dumps and wireless sets.

The Abwehr was divided into three sections: Section I was responsible for obtaining secret information about the enemy; Section II was in charge of operations in enemy territory; Section III was responsible for counter-sabotage and security. This section was the largest branch and was divided into sub-groups. III F, for example, monitored resistance activity and its aim was to infiltrate German agents into resistance networks.

The Gestapo which was distinct from and indeed, in competition with the Abwehr was the shortened term used for Geheime Staats Polizei, (meaning Secret State Police). The Gestapo was a branch of the SicherheitsPolizei or Sipo, which was the security police, and it exerted much control over the populations of the occupied countries. Each major administrative French town had a Gestapo Headquarters. Black Marias, which were windowless vans with a grill on the back door, took resisters and SOE agents from the local prison to the nearest Headquarters.

Each potential recruit to SOE was informed in their interview that their chances of survival in France were 50-50. However, it turned out to be more favourable, with about three in four agents returning from the field. Of those that were caught, however, very few survived imprisonment in concentration camps; most were executed upon arrival or shortly afterwards. Of the 15 F section women who were captured and sent to concentration camps, only Odette Sansom, Yvonne Baseden and Eileen Nearne survived. Of the 100 or so F section men who had been captured, only 16 returned from the camps. Many were in a very poor condition, having suffered both physical and mental torture, as well as malnourishment, hypothermia and a host of other medical ailments.

Yvonne Baseden spent almost a year in King Edward VII's Sanatorium in Midhurst following her release from Ravensbrück concentration camp in 1944. She had TB and before Tudor-Edwards and Price-Thomas could operate on her to remove a lobe out of her right lung which had an abscess on it, she had to be built up so that she would survive the anaesthetic.

ABOVE: *Violette Szabo was taken from this prison in Limoges, twice a day to the Gestapo headquarters which was nearby.*

ABOVE: *The Gestapo Headquarters in Limoges where Violette Szabo was interrogated. The building was taken over by the British, who used it as their headquarters, after the liberation of Limoges.*

ABOVE: *The Third or Women's Division of Fresnes Prison, Paris. Many of the women agents, including Odette Sansom, were imprisoned here.*

Fresnes was a large prison on the outskirts of Paris which was built as a maison de correction to accommodate over 1,600 prisoners. However, it was vastly overcrowded and in the men's section of the prison, five or six shared a cell. Etched on the walls of the cells were defiant and encouraging words such as 'Vive la France' and 'Courage'. Inmates were taken by Black Marias to the Counter Espionage Headquarters at 84 Avenue Foch, by the Arc de Triomphe, for interrogation.

ABOVE: *The entrance of No 84 Avenue Foch, the Counter Espionage Headquarters in Paris. Numerous agents, including Violette Szabo and Odette Sansom, were taken here and tortured.*

At the headquarters, the victim would certainly have been tortured. Most were beaten either by hand, boot or implement. Some had red hot pokers laid upon their body, electric currents attached to their nipples or genitals, electrodes inserted into their vaginas or anuses, their breasts cut off, their fingernails extracted and some experienced the infamous baignoire. A bathtub was filled with water and the victims head was held down inside it almost to the point of drowning. They were then fished out of the water and interrogation continued. Eileen Nearn experienced the baignoire.

RIGHT: *This photograph, discovered in a Gestapo torture chamber in Paris after the Liberation, shows a man cuffed hands and feet, with the back of his knees and his calves gripping a wooden rod, which is balancing on the backs of two chairs. The weight of his body is suspended on the back of his knees and it is likely that he would have been forced to stay in that cramp-inducing position for many hours.*

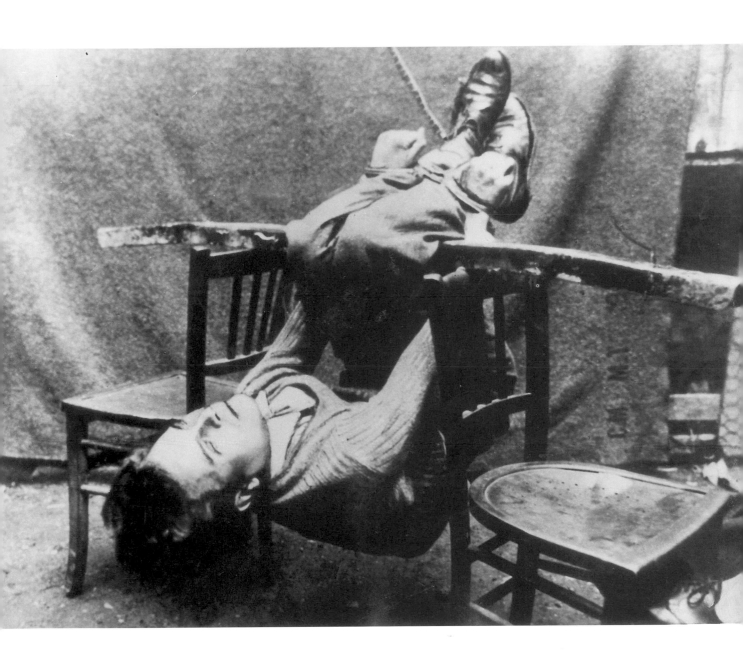

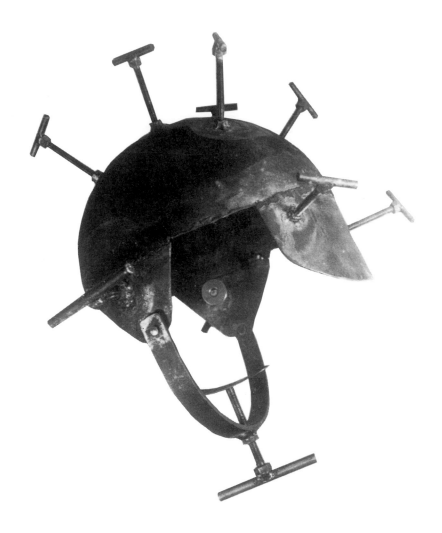

ABOVE: *Implement of torture used on French resisters to try to get them to reveal information. Each of these screws could be tightened to exact more pressure on the scalp. The screw on the bottom of the helmet, attached to the chin-strap, would force the tongue up in the palate of the mouth.*

Many female Jews, resisters, gypsies and political prisoners were sent to Ravensbrück concentration camp for women (Frauenlager). It was situated in the midst of swampland near the village of Ravensbrück, which was close to the resort town of Fürstenburg, 50 miles north of Berlin. It was established in 1938 and was designed to accommodate 6,000 inmates. However, in the last year of the war, it was housing more than 36,000 women. Odette Sansom, Yvonne Baseden and Violette Szabo were just some of the women SOE agents who were imprisoned there. The exact number of women who died at Ravensbrück is unclear, but about 50,000 women, (some sources put the figure as high as 100,000) died from overwork, starvation, overcrowded living conditions, poor sanitation or from medical experiments. The camp was liberated by the Soviets on 1 May 1945. Today, the camp stands as a memorial to those who perished there and many are shocked by the eerie tranquillity which pervades.

ABOVE: *Obersturmbannführer Fritz Sühren, Commandant of Ravensbrück concentration camp for Women. The photograph was found among his private papers.*

BELOW: *Rather than being taken to the local police station before awaiting transportation to a larger prison such as Fresnes, or deportation to a concentration camp, such as Mauthausen, maquisards were often shot immediately. This photograph captures the moment before a number of members of the Lantilly Maquis, based in the Cote D'Or, were massacred on 25 May 1944. The photograph would have been taken by a German soldier as a memento. It is surprising how many photographs and even silent films exist of mass executions committed by German soldiers. This massacre occurred in an open field which reduced the likelihood of a partisan ambush.*

ABOVE: *This photograph, taken on 18 March 1944 in the Saône-et-Loire, shows a number of German soldiers looking at four young maquisards who are awaiting execution. The man whose body is obscured by another maquisard appears to be in conversation with one of the spectating German soldiers who has his hand on his knee.*

RIGHT: *Once killed, their bodies, deprived of a decent burial, were left to rot as this picture illustrates. It shows two members of the Blaimont-Gironde Maquis who had been killed by the Germans.*

LEFT: *Many French resisters were publicly executed as a deterrent to those who participated in clandestine activities. This picture shows a resister who had been tortured, then hanged, at La Mure. He had been a member of the Commune de Vassieux en Vercors. The Vercors was located in-between two departments, the Drome and the Isère, and it was the largest Maquis in France. The ligature around his throat is just visible, but what is peculiar about this execution is that the man pictured was hanged with his feet touching the ground. When he became too tired to prop himself up, the rope tightened around his neck and he strangled himself. This form of execution was much slower than the more usual form of hanging, which resulted in a relatively quick death.*

CHAPTER 11

THE LIBERATION

After D-Day, the Resistance became a much more visible presence in their eagerness to push the Germans out of France. Most pictures which depict Resistance activity date from this period, partly because there was a general feeling that the war was coming to an end and related to this, an eagerness to capture on film wartime friendships and activity. There are numerous pictures of Maquis groups pictured with their arms, as seen on page 177.

Following the D-Day invasion in Normandy on 6 June 1944 and the Allied landings in southern France on the 15 August, Paris was liberated on 25 August. By September 1944, most German Divisions had been driven out of France and there were just a few remaining. The celebrations began almost immediately.

LEFT: *Liberating forces entering the market town of Luzy on 10 September 1944. The French flag is being carried proudly and symbolised the reclaiming of the town as French.*

The Jeds

The Jedburghs were teams of three men who were dropped in uniform into enemy-occupied countries to assist resistance after D-Day. Their purpose was to relay messages from the Allied High Command to local groups and to organise, instruct and arm the maquis. Training was undertaken at Milton Hall, near Peterborough. Lieutenant Colonel FV Spooner was the CO and Oliver Brown, the Chief Instructor, who parachuted into France as the leader of Team Alastair. Oliver Brown's landing was quite spectacular. In his report, he explains that one member of his team hesitated before jumping which meant that they couldn't all jump on the first run. Brown had to wait and jump on the second run with the containers.

'The pilot, believing that he only had packages left in the plane, came down to what must have been about 400 feet and did not de-accelerate at all in dropping, the result being that I got a considerable buffeting, both feet in the rigging lines and took a number of panels out of the chute. One of the maquis who was running to assist me, at the last

ABOVE: *Kenneth Mackenzie of SOE in the centre of the picture heading maquisards into Luzy on 10 September 1944.*

moment, in order to avoid me, lay flat on his stomach, whereupon I sat rather heavily on him, saving myself a considerable amount of discomfort, but rendering him unconscious for two days.'

In total, there were 103 Jedburgh teams and each team was to have at least one British or American Officer and one national of the country. In addition, a wireless operator was assigned to every team. Despite this allocation of roles, each member of the team had been given some training in the other positions, so that the Officer could transmit a message if he was separated from his wireless operator and the operator could assume control if the Officer went missing. The Jed teams were given a name, most of which were men's names, such as Team Alan, Jude, Jacob and Ivor. Many Jeds also went to Burma to join Force 136 which was SOE's Far East branch.

ABOVE: *Having liberated Luzy, some of the 200 members of the Maquis Louis Compagnie (3rd Section) pose with their banners and weapons. Kenneth Macenzie of SOE is in the first row of standing men, fourth from the left.*

LEFT: *Sergeant Alfred Holdham, the wireless operator for Team Jude, pictured with three members of the Resistance. The two women, aged 16, were active in the Resistance and were described as 'very brave'. The two on the right were brother and sister. They are standing in front of a lorry which was used to collect containers parachuted to the group. The Cross of Lorraine is clearly visible on the right wing (to the left of the picture).*

179

EPILOGUE

After the war, justice had to be exercised. On 5 December 1946, the Ravensbrück concentration camp trial began. The dock of No 1 War Crimes Court at Hamburg was filled with the seven German women and nine German men who had all been in positions of authority. Each defendant pleaded not-guilty to the charge 'that they, at Ravensbrück in the years 1939-1945, when members of the staff at Ravensbrück concentration camp, in violation of the laws and usages of war, were concerned in the ill-treatment and killing of allied nationals interned therein.' Major-General VJE Westropp, CBE presided over the court and Major Stephen Stewart led the prosecution, assisted through-out by Squadron Officer Vera Atkins, who had been the Intelligence Officer of SOE's F section. On 16 December 1946, Odette Sansom GC was called as a witness to the prosecution to give her testimony before the court.

ABOVE: *Vera Atkins.*

LEFT: *Staff from Ravensbrück concentration camp in the dock at Hamburg.*

ABOVE: *War Crimes Trial, Hamburg, December 1946. Women shown were all employed at Ravensbrück concentration camp. Front row: Dorothea Binz (executed), Margarette Mewes (10 years imprisonment), Greta Bösel (executed) and Eugenie von Skene (10 years imprisonment). Back row: Elizabeth Marschall (face obscured – executed) and Vera Salvequart (executed). The uniformed woman in the cap is the court official.*

RIGHT: *In 1948, a memorial was unveiled commemorating the 52 FANYs who were killed during the war. This was not restricted to the SOE agents who were executed or died of natural causes. FANYs who had worked at the base stations as wireless operators and coders who had died were also included. The plaque is set in the north wall of St. Paul's Church in Wilton Place, Knightsbridge, London.*

1914 E.F. SHAW CdeG 1918

1939   1945

IN HONOURED MEMORY OF THOSE MEMBERS OF THE
WOMEN'S TRANSPORT SERVICE (F·A·N·Y·)
WHO GAVE THEIR LIVES FOR THEIR KING AND COUNTRY.

M.W. ANDERSON	M. DAMERMENT L d H CdeG	M.L. M·McKENZIE MILLIGAN	E.G. SADLER
Y.E.M. BEEKMAN CdeG	B.M. DICKIE	D. MORGAN	H.J.P. SALMON
D. BLOCH	B.E. EBDEN	R.E. NELSON	J. SHEPLEY
E.M. BOILEAU	M. HEATH-JONES	M.C. PEAKE	L.M. STALKER
A. BORREL	J. HILDICK-SMITH	E.S. PLEWMAN CdeG	E.P. STANGER
M.S. BUTLER	N. INYAT-KHAN GC	B.E. RAMSAY	N.C. STAPYLTON
M. BYCK	C. LEFORT	F.L. RAWLINS	B. SWINBURNE-HANHAM
C.E. CLERK-RATTRAY	V.E. LEIGH	L.V. ROLFE CdeG	V.R.E. SZABO G.C. CdeG
C.D. CROOKE	C.M. LOPRESTI	D.H. ROWDEN CdeG	M.J. THOMPSON
K. CROSS	D.M. MANNING	Y. RUDELLAT	P.C. WOOLLAN
	NEE PORTMAN		(IN JAPAN)

W.T.S. (EAST AFRICA)   C.M. BRADFORD 7·3·1947

B.M. AUSTIN	B. DUNBAR THOMSON.	B. KENTISH	M. SYKES
A. CALLISHER	W. GREY	F.F. MOOJEN	P.H. LE POER TRENCH
H.C. CAMERER		S. HOOK	R. SOUTHEY

THEIR NAME LIVETH FOR EVERMORE.

Odette M. C. HALLOWES GC, MBE, L d H

28 April 1912 - 13 March 1995

Vice-President of W.T.S. (F.A.N.Y.)
1967 - 1995

Here she laid violets,
transforming into service the pain of her survival

Acknowledgements

All the veterans that I have interviewed and in particular, Yvonne Baseden, Alice Bridgewater, Francis Cammaerts, Philip Dawkins, Roger Landes, Milborough Lobonov-Rostovsky, Audrey Rothwell, Margaret Ward, and Cyril Watney, whom I have quoted. Public Records Office, Sound Archives at the Imperial War Museum, Paul Cornish of the Firearms Department at the Imperial War Museum, Royal Signals Museum at Blandford Forum, Dorset, FANY HQ, London, Clive Bassett of RAF Harrington.

Imperial War Museum Photographs:
page 4: hu 2646, 12: mh 24450, 20: hu 28683, 25: hu 3213, 28: hu 16541, 34: hu 28686, 43: hu 67081, 44: hu 53639, 45: hu 66695, 47: hu 66698, 48: mh 24434, 63: mh 1245, 80: mh 1252, 103: hu 47912, 104: hu 56759, 107: hu 56768, 108: hu 56775, 130: hu 56777, 132: mh 11125, 136: mh 11130, 138: mh 11123, 143: hu 53936, 144: hu 57103, 146: hu 59815, 148: hu 49814, 150: mh 11166, 165: mh 11182, 167: mh 11133, 168: hu 70695, 170: hu 68068, 173: hu 68064, 174: hu 68069, 178: hu 62470
All other photographs of agents courtesy of The Special Forces Club, London.
161: Editions Tallandier, 163: collection D.M.P.A.
Other photographs: collection of the author, or specially commissioned by the publishers.

Further Reading

Beryl Escott, 1991, *Mission Improbable: A Salute to the RAF Women of SOE in Wartime France*, Patrick Stephens Ltd, Somerset.
MRD Foot, 1966, *SOE in France*, HMSO, London.
MRD Foot, 1999, *SOE: The Special Operations Executive, 1940-1946*, Pimlico, London.
Patrick Howarth, 1980, *Undercover: The Men and Women of the Special Operations Executive*, Routledge & Kegan Paul, London.
Rita Kramer, 1995, *Flames in the Field: The Story of Four SOE Agents in Occupied France*, Michael Joseph, London.
Leo Marks, 1998, *Between Silk & Cyanide: The Story of SOE's Code War*, HarperCollins Publishers, London.
R.J. Minney, 1956, *Carve Her Name With Pride*, George Newnes, London.
Margaret Pawley, *In Obedience to Instructions: FANY with the SOE in the Mediterranean,* Leo Cooper, Barnsley.
David Stafford, 2000, *Secret Agent: The True Story of the Special Operations Executive*, BBC, London.
Jerrald Tickell, 1949, *Odette: The Story of a British Agent*, Chapman & Hall, London.